# THE BASICS OF PERSONAL PROTECTION IN THE HOME

Produced by the Education & Training Division

A Publication of the National Rifle Association of America

First Edition—September 2000
©2000 The National Rifle Association of America

International Standard Book Number (ISBN): ISBN-10: 0-935998-99-3
ISBN-13: 978-0-935998-99-3

NR40830ES26828 (3-13 Revised)

# ACKNOWLEDGMENTS

The NRA would like to acknowledge the efforts of those whose advice, writing or editing activities contributed to the development of this book:

**Charles Mitchell**, Manager, Training Department, Education & Training Division.

**Larry Quandahl**, Education & Training Division and co-author of the *NRA Guide to the Basics of Personal Protection in the Home.*

**Stanton L. Wormley, Jr.,** NRA Certified Instructor and author of the *NRA Guide to the Basics of Personal Protection in the Home.*

The NRA would also like to thank the many staff members, their families and friends who modeled for photographs in this book, including:

| | |
|---|---|
| Dave Adams | Susan Pandis |
| Carla Adams | Naomi Quandahl |
| Gloria Brooks | Larry Quandahl |
| Rudy DuFour | Stela Sipes |
| Rob Farmer | Mark Weaver |
| Grace Lee | Stanton Wormley, Jr. |
| Scott Mayer | Kathy Zimmerman |
| Susan Mayer | |

Additionally, the NRA would like to thank the many NRA Certified Instructors, NRA staff, NRA members and others too numerous to mention whose assistance helped make this book possible.

# TABLE OF CONTENTS

# SAFETY NOTE

The primary rule of gun safety is, "**ALWAYS** keep the firearm pointed in a safe direction." Implicit in that is the notion that a firearm must never be pointed at another human being (except, of course, in a self-defense situation). This rule must always be observed; it cannot be relaxed even for legitimate education or training purposes.

Many of the photographs in this book illustrate defensive firearm use, or specific shooting stances or positions. For instructional purposes it often was necessary to position the camera in front of the muzzle of the gun, or to re-create defensive scenarios in which the home defender would point his or her firearm at an attacker. *At no time was an actual functioning firearm used in these photographs.* When it was necessary to depict a home defender pointing a firearm at an assailant, a solid plastic, non-firing training gun was used. In other photographs in which the camera was located forward of the muzzle, special deactivated, non-firing training guns were employed.

Absolute, unvarying adherence to this first and most important of gun safety rules cannot be overstressed. Real guns—even when clearly unloaded—must never be used in re-creating or practicing home defense scenarios, or in any other training activity in which the firearm may be pointed at a training partner or other person. If you engage in such activities, always use a non-firing training gun designed for that purpose.

# INTRODUCTION

As a result of the increase in crime that began in the 1980s, recent years have seen an increased public interest in every aspect of self-defense and personal protection. Enrollment in martial-arts classes has soared, sales of home and vehicle security systems are at an all-time high, and interest in self-defense handguns and firearms training has never been greater. A sign of the public concern with personal safety has been the passage (in more than 40 states as of this writing) of laws permitting law-abiding citizens the right to carry a concealed firearm.

For many, the term *personal protection* immediately evokes images of martial-arts techniques or a handgun in a nightstand. In truth, however, the use of force is only one of many methods that you can employ to defend life and limb, and indeed is used only as a last resort, when other methods have failed. For myriad ethical, legal and practical reasons, it is always preferable to escape, evade, deter or otherwise avoid an attack rather than be forced to counter it with force. Even when planning and skill give you an overwhelming advantage over an assailant, sidestepping a violent confrontation is always the best course. Furthermore, many states have laws requiring you to retreat as much as is safely possible before using force to defend yourself or others (although in most states you do not have a "duty to retreat" in home defense situations, which are the focus of this book).

There are times, however, when circumstances allow no other option but the use of force to save your life or the lives of your family members. Under such circumstances, a firearm—most commonly, a handgun—is unquestionably the most effective defensive tool available, if it is used properly. The ability to use a firearm effectively is not something you are born with; it must be developed through the mastery of a series of interlocking skills, and then must be reinforced through frequent practice.

*The Basics of Personal Protection in the Home* is unique among personal protection handbooks in that it addresses both aspects of a total personal protection strategy in the home. Much of the book deals with techniques and strategies designed to deter burglars, home invaders and other criminals. Included are ways to make your home less appealing to professional criminals, who will be inclined to seek easier targets. This information alone will be of value to many, especially those who have chosen not to have firearms in their homes.

Homeowners who do incorporate a handgun into their personal protection strategy will also find much value in this book, including chapters on shooting positions, aiming and firing techniques, the use of cover and concealment, and methods of clearing various types of malfunctions. These skills and others presented in this book form the core shooting skills used to counter a life-threatening attack in the home.

The Basics of Personal Protection in the Home is divided into six parts: Safety; Mental Preparation; Developing Defensive Shooting Skills; Strategies for Home and Personal Safety; Firearms, Self-Defense and the Law; and Selecting Firearms, Ammunition and Accessories for Personal Protection. Also included are appendices on firearm maintenance, resources for additional information, and facts about the NRA.

Although this book has a wealth of information on virtually every aspect of personal protection in the home, it is meant to be used within the framework of the NRA Basic Personal Protection in the Home Course, a hands-on program encompassing 8 hours of classroom and range instruction. (Mastery of the shooting skills, such as those taught in the NRA Basic Pistol Course is a prerequisite for this course.) You should understand that merely reading a book—any book—will not, in and of itself, make you proficient at the various skills involved in home defense. For more information on the NRA Basic Personal Protection in the Home Course or any other NRA course, call (703) 267-1423.

## A Gun Owner's Responsibilities

Americans enjoy a right that citizens of many other countries do not–the right to own firearms. But with this right comes a responsibility. It is the gun owner's responsibility to store, operate and maintain his or her firearms safely. It is the gun owner's responsibility to ensure that unauthorized or untrained individuals cannot gain access to his or her firearms. And it is the gun owner's responsibility to learn and obey all applicable laws that pertain to the purchase, possession and use of a firearm in his or her locale. Guns are neither safe nor unsafe by themselves. When people learn and practice responsible gun ownership, firearms are safe.

# PART I:
# SAFETY

# CHAPTER 1

# BASIC FIREARM SAFETY

Safety is fundamental to all shooting activities. Whether you're practicing at the range, cleaning your gun in your workshop, or defending your family from an attack, the rules of firearm safety always apply.

Safe gun handling involves the development of knowledge, skills and attitudes—knowledge of the gun safety rules, the skill to apply these rules, and a safety-first attitude that arises from a sense of responsibility and a knowledge of potential dangers.

Though there are many specific principles of safe firearm handling and operation, all are derived from just three basic gun safety rules.

## FUNDAMENTAL RULES OF FIREARM SAFETY

ALWAYS **keep the gun pointed in a safe direction.** This is the primary rule of gun safety. A *safe direction* means that the gun is pointed so that even if it were to go off, it would not cause injury or damage. The key to this rule is to control where the muzzle or front end of the barrel is pointed at all times. Common sense dictates the safest direction, depending upon the circumstances. If only this one safety rule were always followed, there would be no injuries or fatalities from accidental shootings.

ALWAYS **keep your finger off the trigger until ready to shoot.** Your trigger finger should always be kept straight, alongside the frame and out of the trigger guard, until you have made the decision to shoot.

When holding a gun, many people have a tendency to place their finger on the trigger, even when they are not ready to shoot. This is an extremely dangerous practice. Many negligent discharges are caused when the trigger of a loaded gun is inadvertently pressed by a finger carelessly left in the trigger guard instead of being positioned straight along the side of the gun's frame.

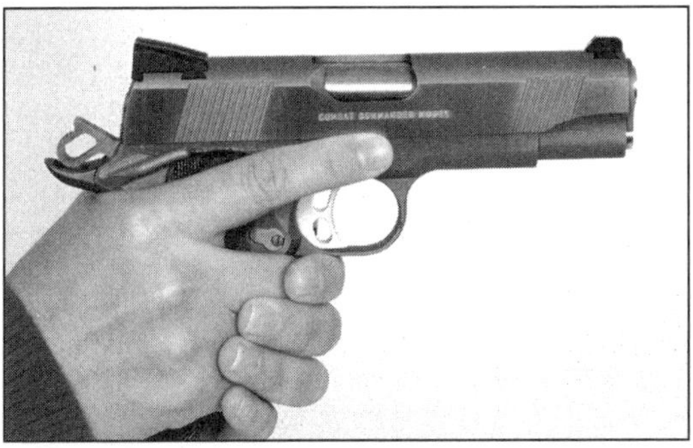

*Fig. 1. ALWAYS* **keep your finger off the trigger until you are ready to shoot.** *The trigger finger should be placed alongside the gun's frame.*

3

**ALWAYS** keep the firearm unloaded until ready to use. A firearm that is not being used should always be unloaded. For example, at the range, your firearm should be left unloaded while you walk downrange and check your target. Similarly, a firearm that is being stored in a gun safe or lock box should generally be unloaded (unless it is a personal protection firearm that may need to be accessed quickly for defensive purposes—see Chapter 2: Defensive Shooting Safety).

As a general rule, whenever you pick up a gun, point it in a safe direction with your finger off the trigger, engage the safety (if the gun is equipped with one), remove the magazine (if the gun is equipped with a removable magazine), and then open the action and look into the chamber(s) to determine if the gun is loaded or not. Unless the firearm is being kept in a state of readiness for personal protection, it should be unloaded. If you do not know how to open the action or inspect the firearm, leave the gun alone and get help from someone who does, and consult the owner's manual that came with the gun.

*Fig. 2. ALWAYS* keep the firearm unloaded until you are ready to use it.

# RULES FOR USING OR STORING A GUN

In addition to these three basic firearm safety rules, you must follow a number of additional rules when you use or store your firearm.

**Know your target and what is beyond.** Whether you are at the range, in the woods, or in your home, if you're going to shoot you must know what lies beyond your target. In almost all cases, you must be sure that there is something that will serve as a backstop to capture bullets that miss or go through the target. Never fire in a direction in which there are innocent people or any other potential for mishap. Think first, shoot second.

**Know how to use the gun safely**. Before handling a gun, learn how it operates. Read the owner's manual for your gun. Contact the gun's manufacturer for an owner's manual if you do not have one. Know your gun's basic parts, how to safely open and close the action, and how to remove ammunition from the gun. No matter how much you know about guns, you must always take the time to learn the proper way to operate any new or unfamiliar firearm. Never assume that because one gun resembles another, they both operate in exactly the same way. Also, remember a gun's mechanical safety device is never foolproof. Guidance in safe gun operation should be obtained from the owner's manual or a qualified gunsmith.

**Be sure your gun is safe to operate.** Just like other tools, guns need regular maintenance to remain operable. Regular cleaning and proper storage are a part of the gun's general upkeep. If there is any question regarding a gun's ability to function, it should be examined by a knowledgeable gunsmith. Proper maintenance procedures may be found in your owner's manual, as well as in Appendix A: Firearm Maintenance.

**Use only the correct ammunition for your gun.** Each firearm is intended for use with a specific cartridge. Only cartridges designed for a particular gun can be fired safely in that gun. Most guns have the ammunition type stamped on the barrel and/or slide. The owner's manual will also list the cartridge or cartridges appropriate for your gun. Ammunition can be identified by information printed on the cartridge box and sometimes stamped on the cartridge head. Do not shoot the gun unless you know you have the proper ammunition.

**Wear eye and ear protection as appropriate.** The sound of a gunshot can damage unprotected ears. Gun discharges can also emit debris and hot gas that could cause eye injury. Thus, both ear and eye protection are highly recommended (if possible) whenever you are firing live ammunition in your gun. Safety glasses and ear plugs or muffs should also be worn by any spectators or shooting partners present during live-fire sessions. Obviously, during

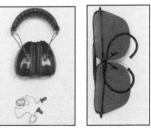

*Fig. 3. Ear protection (l.) and eye protection should be worn whenever you shoot, if possible.*

an actual violent encounter necessitating the use of your firearm, it likely will not be possible for you to use eye and ear protection.

**Never use alcohol or drugs before or while shooting.** Alcohol and many drugs can impair normal mental and physical bodily functions, sharply diminishing your ability to shoot safely. These substances must never be used before or while handling or shooting guns.

Note that these effects are produced not just by illegal or prescription drugs. Many over-the-counter medications also have considerable side effects, which may be multiplied when certain drugs are taken together or with alcohol. Read the label of any medication you take, no matter how innocuous, or consult your physician or pharmacist for possible side effects. If the label advises against driving or operating equipment while taking the medication, you should also avoid using a firearm while taking it.

**Store guns so they are inaccessible to unauthorized persons.** It is your responsibility as a gun owner to take reasonable steps to prevent unauthorized persons (especially children) from handling or otherwise having access to your firearms. You have a number of options for accomplishing this, which are discussed in greater detail in Chapter 3: Safe Firearm Storage. The particular storage method you choose will be based upon your own particular home situation and security needs.

**Be aware that certain types of guns and many shooting activities require additional safety precautions.** There are many different types of firearms, some of which require additional safety rules or procedures for proper operation. These are commonly found in your firearm's owner's manual. Also, most sport shooting activities have developed a set of rules to ensure safety during competition. These rules are generally sport-specific; the procedures for loading your firearm and commencing fire, for example, are different in NRA bullseye shooting than they are in NRA Action Pistol competition (see Chapter 12: Opportunities for Skills Enhancement).

---

## SAFETY NOTE

Many of the photographs in this book illustrate defensive firearm use, or specific shooting stances or positions. For instructional purposes it often was necessary to position the camera in front of the muzzle of the gun, or to re-create defensive scenarios in which the home defender would point his or her firearm at an attacker. **At no time was an actual functioning firearm used in these photographs.** When it was necessary to depict a home defender pointing a firearm at an assailant, a solid plastic, non-firing training gun was used. In other photographs in which the camera was forward of the muzzle, deactivated, non-firing training guns were used.

Real guns—even when clearly unloaded—must never be used in re-creating or practicing home defense scenarios, or in any other activity in which the firearm may be pointed at a training partner or other person. For such activities, always use a non-firing training gun designed for that purpose.

---

The Basics of Personal Protection in the Home

# CHAPTER 2

# DEFENSIVE SHOOTING SAFETY

The gun safety rules in the preceding chapter are applicable whenever a gun is handled or fired. However, some of these rules need to be reinforced in light of the particular dynamics and characteristics of defensive shooting situations.

Probably the greatest obstacle to safe gun handling in defensive situations is stress. In the overwhelming confusion of a violent encounter, it is easy to forget or disregard even the most basic gun safety rules. After all, when you are being attacked, your entire being is focused upon just one thing: survival. You may be totally unaware that when you swung your pistol around to aim at an assailant, you momentarily pointed your loaded firearm at your spouse or your children.

*Keeping a gun pointed in a safe direction* is fairly easy when at the range. Generally, pointing the gun downrange is safe. In a home, however, when facing an aggressive attack, a safe direction may be harder to identify. Under such conditions, a safe direction means more than just

*Fig. 4. This basement contains many items at which a gun should never be pointed, including a kerosene heater, a fuse box, flammable liquids, a water heater, an exterior window, and the family pet.*

pointing a firearm away from loved ones and innocent bystanders. For example, it is also unsafe to point a firearm at propane gas tanks, oil tanks, kerosene heaters and other objects containing flammable materials. Pointing a firearm at a window is also unsafe, as any bullet that is discharged might hit an innocent bystander outside. The determination of what is a "safe direction" in a particular home has to be made after a consideration of many factors, such as the building layout, composition of wall materials, the location of family members or other persons and the presence of flammable or penetrable items.

In anticipation of the need to fire quickly during an encounter with an aggressor, many people unconsciously hold their firearm with their finger on the trigger, even when they are not intending to fire immediately. This violation of a basic rule of safety—*ALWAYS* **keep your finger off the trigger until ready to shoot**—can have disastrous consequences, as the stress of a real or potential attack can make you prone to an involuntary, reflexive muscular contraction if suddenly startled. It is easy to imagine the tragic result if you inadvertently pointed your firearm at a loved one or an innocent bystander when such a preventable discharge should occur.

As was explained in the previous chapter, it is a basic rule of gun safety that *a firearm should be kept unloaded until ready to use*. In the context of personal protection, "ready to use" means more than merely "ready to shoot." A self-defense firearm you keep in your home is "ready to use" throughout the entire period you are there; a gun you keep in a nightstand next to your bed is "ready to use" during the hours you spend at night in your bedroom. When you are not in your home, however, the firearm kept there is no longer ready to be used by you, and must then be kept unloaded and secured, to prevent access by an inquisitive child or other unauthorized person.

One of the most important— and problematic—safety rules in

*Fig. 5. Knowing your target is critical. What looks like the silhouette of a man with a club in the doorway (left) may actually be a yawning family member coming to bed with a magazine.*

relation to defensive shooting situations is *know your target and what is beyond.* Knowing your target is critical to prevent shooting a family member, neighbor's child, police officer or other innocent person who may enter or be in your home without your knowledge. Safety, ethics and the law dictate that you identify your target and verify it is a lethal and imminent threat before you fire.

*Knowing what is beyond your target* is also critical. In the stress of an

The Basics of Personal Protection in the Home

*Fig. 6. It is critical to be aware of what is beyond your target. Here a home defender has become so focused on an attacker coming through the door that she has lost awareness of the children and houses in the background that could be endangered if she should shoot.*

aggressive attack, you cannot assume that all of your shots will hit your target. Also, depending upon the gun and ammunition you are using, the range over which shooting takes place, the size and dress of your attacker, and the location of your hits on your attacker, some of your bullets may completely penetrate your assailant and continue on, presenting danger to persons or objects beyond.

In your home, you can minimize the potential danger of bullets that miss or pass through by preselecting your firing positions so that solid walls or other effective backstops are behind your target. It is not practical to do this while in the heat of an attack, so identifying such lanes of fire should be part of the defensive plan for your home and family (see Chapter 13: Making You and Your Home Safer). For example, when establishing a safe room in your home, try to choose a room and a firing position in that room such that, should you have to fire through the doorway of that room at an incoming aggressor, a thick wall, steel safe, or other object can serve as a backstop.

Gun safety must also be observed while you are honing your firearm skills, whether you're shooting live ammunition at the range or performing dry-fire practice at home. Specific safety precautions for these activities are outlined in Chapter 12: Opportunities for Skills Enhancement.

It may seem unrealistic to expect a person undergoing an attack to be conscious of the gun safety rules, much less adhere to them. Through constant repetition and mindfulness, however, safe gun handling can become gun safety habits that function automatically even during the stress of a violent encounter.

# CHAPTER 3

# SAFE FIREARM STORAGE

Safe gun storage is an integral part of gun safety. It is one of your prime responsibilities as a gun owner to take all reasonable precautions to prevent unauthorized persons from having access to your firearms. By storing your firearms safely, you not only avoid the possibility of an accidental shooting involving a child or other untrained person; you may also prevent a criminal from using your firearm against an innocent person, including members of your own family.

In addition, some jurisdictions have laws mandating secure firearm storage. Almost all jurisdictions have criminal negligence laws that can be applied to gun owners who do not take reasonable precautions in storing their firearms.

*Fig. 7. A lockable gun box is one option to prevent unauthorized access to a stored firearm.*

There are two main requirements for the storage of defensive firearms. First and foremost, the storage method chosen must provide an adequate level of protection to prevent unauthorized persons from accessing the firearms. The determination of what is "adequate protection" is a matter of judgment on the part of the gun owner. What is adequate in a home inhabited by a single person or a couple with no children might be wholly inadequate in a home in which numerous adults or children reside.

The second requirement is that the storage method or device used must allow the gun to be easily retrieved as needed to defend against an intruder or an attack. Again, "easily retrieved" depends upon the particular circumstances of the environment.

Defensive firearm storage usually involves a compromise between the two requirements presented above. Storage methods that provide a high level of security, for example, often do not allow quick and easy firearm access. Often, the gun owner is best served by utilizing more than one storage method, allowing adaptation to different needs and situations.

There is no one best method of firearm storage nor one best type of locking or storage device. Each has advantages and limitations. You must choose the firearm storage method that is best for you given your circumstances and preferences.

It is also incumbent upon you as a responsible, law-abiding gun owner to know and observe all applicable state and local laws regarding safe gun storage. For example, if the law in your jurisdiction requires a trigger lock on all stored guns, you must abide by that law no matter what other storage methods you also use, such as a high-security gun safe.

# TYPES OF LOCKING MECHANISMS

All storage methods designed to prevent unauthorized access utilize some sort of locking mechanism. Different types of locking mechanisms offer varying degrees of security and accessibility. *Keyed locks*, such as padlocks and the lockable drawers of desks and nightstands, can offer a reasonable level of security (depending upon the construction of the lock and the storage device). However, under stress or in darkness it may be difficult for some to locate the correct key or to manipulate it in the lock. A lesser concern, but one worth mentioning, is that inserting and turning a key in a gun box lock would likely create some sound—whether it is keys jingling together on a key ring or the movement of the lock's tumblers— that could alert a stealthily approaching intruder.

*Combination locks* are often found on gun storage boxes, and range from simple triple-rotary-tumbler models to units that rival the mechanisms found on bank vaults. For many people, combination locks are both secure and familiar to operate. Under stress, however, lock combinations can be confused or forgotten by the gun owner, and the tumblers can be challenging to manipulate quickly and accurately. Also, in darkness or even dim light, combination locks can be virtually impossible to operate, making them less than optimal for devices used for emergency firearm storage.

*Simplex®-type locks* provide a good combination of security and quick access. Such locks feature a number of buttons that are pushed in a specific order to open the device. With only minimal practice, these locks can be easily worked in total darkness. Locks having Simplex-type mechanisms can be just as strong and tamper-resistant as any other.

Another advantage of a Simplex lock is that incorrect entry blocks any further attempt to open the lock. A separate clearing code must be entered before the lock will accept the correct combination, making this lock even more resistant to unauthorized attempts to open it.

The basic Simplex-type lock is a mechanical lock, and thus does not depend upon house current or batteries. Some locking devices, however,

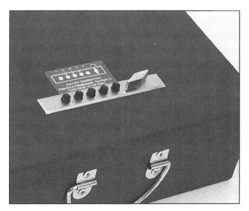

combine Simplex principles with modern electronics. Typically, the storage device features a numeric keypad whose numbered buttons are pushed in a specific order to unlock. A variation on this involves five fingerpads, ergonomically placed on the top or front of the device, which can easily be felt in the dark and which are pressed in a sequence (such as thumb, middle finger, little finger, ring finger) to open the device. It is important to note that such locking mechanisms are

*Fig. 8. A Simplex®-type lock consists of a series of buttons that are pressed in a specific order to open the box. An advantage of this type of gun box is that the lock can be opened in the dark by feel.*

usually disabled when electric power is lost (as from dead batteries or a failure in house current). There usually is a provision for opening the box with a key under such circumstances, but this could be problematic under stress or in the dark.

## TYPES OF STORAGE DEVICES

As mentioned previously, there are many different methods for storing firearms safely, several of which may fit into your defensive plan.

*Gun cases* are commonly used for the transportation and casual storage of firearms. Gun cases are typically of synthetic material, though some more costly models are made of aluminum. Some have integral locks; others feature hasps for small keyed or combination padlocks.

Gun cases can be useful in several ways. Where it is legal to transport your gun by air or other common carrier, it must be in a gun case; some specific requirements as to the type and construction of the case may apply. Also, Federal law mandates that a gun

*Fig. 9. A plastic gun case secured with a padlock that locks both handles of the case together.*

transported across state lines in your vehicle must be in a "locked container" (such as a gun case) when it cannot be transported in a compartment separate from the driver's compartment. Some states also have additional requirements for transporting guns within state boundaries. Even in jurisdictions or situations in which guns need not be transported in a gun case, it is still a good idea to do so, both to keep them out of sight and to protect them from being jostled together or damaged in your trunk, truck box and so forth. In the home, gun cases serve to protect firearms from dust and moisture. Often, guns kept in gun safes for long-term or permanent storage are first put into gun cases.

Handguns are often stored in pistol *lock boxes*. Typically, such boxes are made of steel and feature integral keyed, combination or Simplex-type locks; a few have electronic numeric keypads or fingerpads. Lock boxes are effective in preventing unauthorized access in low-to-moderate security environments, such as a home in which the primary threat is from inquisitive children.

*Fig. 10. A pistol lock box with a Simplex-type lock.*

Some lock boxes are designed to store a gun securely out of sight while also providing quick access to that gun if it is needed for defensive purposes. Such boxes are typically located in desk drawers, under countertops or the kneewells of desks, in nightstands and other unobtrusive locations, and may be held in place with screws or bolts that can be accessed only when the box is open. Quick-access boxes usually feature locks of the Simplex, electronic keypad or fingerpad type. Many novel mechanisms exist to provide quick access once the box is opened, from harnesses that swing out and present the gun grip-first to platforms that slide out for easy access.

*Gun safes* are designed to offer the greatest level of safety for your guns. Upper-end models provide walls and doors that are virtually impossible to defeat by brute force, high-security mechanical or electronic locks, and complex locking patterns that fasten the door to the frame in multiple locations with thick, hardened steel pins. Most of these models are too heavy and bulky for thieves to carry away easily, even when they are not bolted to the floor; some also offer a degree of fire protection.

Although appropriate for permanent firearm storage, gun safes may not be the best choice for the temporary storage of guns that may need to be quickly retrieved. The weight and size of gun safes often consigns them to the basement of a house, far from your safe room. Even when located in the safe room, the combination locks and heavy bolting mechanisms typical of such devices make it difficult to access your gun quickly and quietly. Even when equipped with a lighted keypad for quicker access, the sound of the handle being turned and the locking pins retracting will unquestionably alert an intruder in a quiet house.

There are a few alternative storage methods that should also be mentioned. Many people store guns in a lockable drawer of a desk, nightstand, file cabinet or the like. Arguably, in a home in which it is safe to do so, a loaded defensive firearm kept in a nightstand by the bed could be kept in an unlocked drawer while the gun owner is actually in the bedroom for rapid access in a life-threatening situation. The

*Fig. 11. A typical full-size gun safe will have sufficient capacity to store a number of handguns and long guns, as well as items such as cameras, jewelry, and other valuables.*

decision to store a gun in this manner must be reached after a careful consideration of the circumstances, needs and risks involved.

Also available are lockable racks allowing firearms (particularly long guns) to be displayed or stored openly. These feature a locking bar that passes through the trigger guard, around the frame and so forth, and is secured by a keyed or combination lock. Since such racks do not protect a gun from moisture, dust, or fingerprints, and do not conceal a gun from prying eyes, they are best mounted in a locked gun room or gun closet.

Though not actually suitable for gun storage, there are a number of quick-access devices that orient a handgun for a fast grab. Some of these devices are designed for nighttime use, and orient a gun in a grip-upward position alongside the mattress. Others place a handgun in a horizontal position directly under a counter, drawer or desktop. These items may be useful in high-threat environments in which there may be no time to work even a Simplex-type lock—an environment in which life or death may hinge on immediate access to a firearm.

# SUMMARY

No single storage method is best. The responsible gun owner will use a mixture of storage methods—gun cases for transportation to and from the range, a hidden lock box for in-home quick access, and a gun safe for high-security storage of other firearms—to restrict unauthorized access while facilitating easy retrieval when necessary. Research into the various storage options, and a carefully thought-out defensive plan, will help you decide which firearm storage options are appropriate for your situation.

# PART II:
# MENTAL PREPARATION

# CHAPTER 4

# AWARENESS

An awareness of your environment and the real or potential threats that may be in it is one of the most important keys to staying safe, whether at home or on the street. Such an awareness can help you avoid a violent confrontation altogether, or can give you more time to prepare an effective response to an attack that cannot be averted. Remember, it is always best to evade a confrontation by any means possible. Deadly force should be used only as a last resort when no other option is available.

To help in evaluating your alertness at any time, it is useful to identify several different levels of awareness. Readers with military or police experience or prior practical training may have been exposed to this in the form of a four- or five-step "color code" of tactical awareness. The NRA utilizes four levels of awareness: *unaware*, *aware*, *alert*, and *alarm*.

## UNAWARE

Much of the average person's time in and around the home or business is spent in an *unaware* condition—a condition in which *one is not alert to the immediate environment.*

The ultimate state of unawareness, of course, is sleep, but an unaware state is also common during activities that require attention or concentration, such as watching television, driving a car, carrying on a conversation, reading a book, preparing a meal or doing household chores. People are also often unaware of their surroundings when they are deep in thought or

*Fig. 12. A person in an **unaware** state. Her headphones prevent her from hearing any suspicious noise, and she is oblivious to what is going on outside her front door.*

daydreaming, or when they are in the grip of intense emotions. An unaware state (or, at best, a state of markedly reduced awareness) can additionally be caused by fatigue or illness, alcohol, and the use of both illegal and legal drugs (including many over-the-counter medications).

Being in an unaware condition is probably inescapable at least some of the time. Nonetheless, from a practical point of view, unawareness is to be avoided as much as possible, for such a state lessens the likelihood that a threat will be perceived or recognized, and also slows your response to danger even after it has been identified. Many criminal attacks are planned for times and circumstances in which the victim feels safe and protected, and is thus likely to be in a state of unawareness.

# AWARE

In the *aware* state, a person is *conscious of his or her surroundings, and of those persons around him or her*. However, at this stage, he or she has not identified potential threats in the environment.

Awareness can involve any of the senses, including sight, hearing, smell and touch; sight and hearing, however, are the most useful in perceiving threats in your environment. Under conditions in which a potential threat is likely to be present, the prudent person avoids anything that may impair the acuity of the eyes or ears. Wearing stereo headphones while walking along the street or working in your yard may help the time pass more pleasantly, but also prevents you from detecting the sound of an assailant's footsteps approaching from behind.

While it is relatively easy to operate at a condition of heightened awareness for short periods, particularly under conditions in which a threat is likely, it is much more difficult to maintain that awareness for an extended length of time in environments that seem protected or safe, such as your home or office.

There is a considerable difference between having a general awareness of the threats that may lurk in your environment, and a

*Fig. 13. A person in an **aware** state. Note that she has removed her personal stereo headphones, and is taking a moment to observe her environment.*

feeling of paranoia or excessive vigilance. Just as a skillful and experienced driver automatically and effortlessly perceives and responds to potential collisions and other road hazards, you can develop an unforced, unconscious alertness to your surroundings.

The Basics of Personal Protection in the Home

# ALERT

An individual at the *alert* level has *identified a specific potential threat or threats*. This is in contrast to the *aware* state, in which one has only a generalized consciousness of all those things in the environment that could be a source of a threat.

Potential or hypothetical threats may originate from many sources. Often, certain types of people are perceived as threatening or intimidating.

*Fig. 14. A person in an **alert** state. She has identified a specific potential threat in her environment (a man in a ski mask). Her actions should include planning a course of action, and setting a threshhold stimulus that will initiate that plan.*

Relying upon stereotypical images to gauge the likelihood of a violent encounter can sometimes make one vulnerable to other, unexpected sources of danger. A homeowner may keep a wary eye on a group of rowdy teenagers on the corner, and as a result, be totally oblivious to a middle-aged assailant neatly dressed in a coat and tie.

Even in the apparent absence of other people, many possible threats in the environment remain. A clump of bushes, an unlocked garage or a darkened porch may all conceal a violent assailant. Any unusual or out-of-the-ordinary occurrence, such as an outdoor security light that is inexplicably broken, may also signal a potential threat lurking in the darkness. With practice, you can become more adept at identifying such dangers.

In the home, a specific potential threat may take many forms:

- a knock on the door;
- the approach of a stranger;
- an unexpected noise;
- a door-to-door salesperson, solicitor or survey taker;
- a stranger asking for assistance, or to use the telephone; or
- an unfamiliar car with people inside, parked in front of your house.

As a general rule, any person not known to the residents of the house constitutes a potential threat, no matter who they seem or claim to be.

Remember that the alert level involves identification of a specific potential threat, not a real or actual threat. Not every unidentified sound indicates a housebreaker; not every stranger at the door has criminal intent.

It is crucial at the alert level of awareness to take two steps immediately after identifying a specific potential threat. Step One is to formulate a hypothetical plan of action to respond to the threat. This plan is absolutely essential; it is always quicker to act than to react. The planned response can be the evasion of an attack—by means of avoidance, flight, issuing a verbal warning, alerting the police and so on—or, as a last resort, the employment of force to defend yourself or your family. Implicit in this plan is not only what course of action will be taken (as in, "I will flee from an intruder") but also how ("I will escape out of my back door and immediately go to my neighbor's house"). Of course, the plan must be flexible enough to allow you to respond to changing circumstances. Depending upon your attacker's behavior, you may have to shift between the "evasive" and "defensive" modes of action.

It is always important to have more than one plan of action. Plans rarely unfold as anticipated, and having one or more contingency plans may mean the difference between life and death. It is essential to keep thinking and planning, to be continually alert to opportunities that present themselves, and to be flexible enough to adapt your plan of action to changing circumstances.

Note that your plan of action does not have to involve the use of force. Most responses to an attack fall into one of two broad categories: evasion or defense. Evasion, if safely possible, is preferable. As has been stated above, and as is repeated numerous times in this text, the best course of action is to avoid or evade a violent confrontation altogether. The use of force, deadly or otherwise, should be regarded only as a last resort.

Even when force is used in self-defense, opportunities for evasion may subsequently arise. Your plan should take into account chances that may arise to safely flee a confrontation at any time.

Step Two is to establish a "threshold stimulus" that will initiate the plan of action. Once the potential threat has crossed that threshold, the next level of awareness, *alarm*, is reached and the plan immediately goes into effect. A threshold stimulus may be many things: the approach of a potential threat within a certain distance; the refusal of a threat to depart when told to leave; the presentation of a weapon by the threat; an overt gesture or statement from the threat indicating an intention to do harm, and so forth.

# ALARM

At the *alarm* level of awareness, the specific potential threat identified in the *alert* stage has *crossed one or more of the thresholds previously established, and has become a real threat to your safety.* Your senses are

*Fig. 15. Once a threat has crossed the threshhold stimulus and has gone from being a potential threat to an actual threat, the home defender enters the **alarm** stage. In this stage, the course of action planned in the alert stage is now implemented (in this case, calling the police and retreating to an upstairs safe room).*

heightened, and you will likely feel a high level of fear and anxiety. The course of action planned in the *alert* stage is now implemented.

Often it is appropriate to establish a cascade of stimuli that sets into motion an escalating sequence of actions. For example, a homeowner might establish the following sequence of stimuli and actions to respond to an unidentified sound in the middle of the night:

- *Threshhold Stimulus:* Occurrence of suspicious sounds (*alert* level).
- *First Action:* Retreat to safe room and acquire firearm.
- *Second Action:* Establish next threshhold stimulus and plan response to that stimulus.

- *Second Threshhold Stimulus:* Recurrence of suspicious sounds (*alarm* level).
- *First Action:* Call police.
- *Second Action:* Establish next threshhold stimulus and plan response to that stimulus.

- *Third Threshhold Stimulus:* Approach of intruder toward safe room.
- *First Action:* Issue verbal warning for intruder to leave.
- *Second Action:* Establish next threshhold stimulus and plan response to that stimulus.

- *Fourth Threshhold Stimulus:* Intruder ignores warning and enters safe room with a weapon.
- *Action:* Utilize firearm to stop intruder.

## SUMMARY

As is stressed many times in this handbook, the use of a firearm or other deadly weapon to protect yourself should be an act of last resort, when no other option is available. It is always better to escape, evade, avoid or deter an attack than to resolve it through the use of force. By employing your powers of awareness—one of the most important personal protection tools you possess—you will be able to recognize threats in your environment early on, which in turn may enable you to escape or avoid them. If you fail to maintain a state of awareness, you are more likely to become a victim of an attack, or to have to use deadly force to defend yourself.

# CHAPTER 5

# THE DEFENSIVE MINDSET

As was discussed in Chapter 4, you are often able to avoid or evade violent confrontations through an awareness of the potential threats in your environment. In some situations, however, an attack cannot be averted. Surviving such situations depends not only upon using the appropriate defensive and practical skills, but also upon having a defensive mindset. Your *defensive mindset* consists of the values, mental techniques, and attitude that maximize the effectiveness of your response to an assault. These attributes also influence the effectiveness of your training regimen, so the development of a defensive mindset is an important initial stage in the NRA Basic Personal Protection in the Home Course.

## WILLINGNESS TO USE FORCE IN SELF-DEFENSE

The NRA Basic Personal Protection in the Home Course teaches the law-abiding citizen how to use a handgun for personal protection when threatened with deadly force in the home. This entails training to shoot an assailant as a last resort, if necessary. A person having moral, religious or personal objections to using deadly force and possibly taking a life should not incorporate a firearm into his or her personal protection strategy.

Anyone contemplating the inclusion of a firearm in a personal protection strategy must consider the following questions:
- *Am I prepared to take the life of another human being to save my own or my family's?*
- *Does my religion permit the taking of a life in self-defense?*
- *Do my personal moral standards permit the taking of a life in self-defense?*
- *Am I prepared to tolerate the judgment of my family, friends and neighbors if I must defend myself with lethal force?*

Even when it is necessary and justified, shooting a violent criminal is not a pleasant experience. This should be realized and planned for as part of your mental training.

The *willingness* to take a life in self-defense is very different from the *desire* to take a life. No responsible, decent person enjoys taking a life, no matter how depraved or malignant the assailant may be. The willingness to use deadly force in self-defense does not imply a devaluation of human life. In fact, those who include a firearm in their personal protection plans are affirming the value of their own lives and those of their family members. The ethical person does not ever want to use deadly force, but recognizes that there are times when it may be the only option to protect innocent lives.

## DETERMINATION TO NEVER GIVE UP

There's an old country saying that runs something like this: "It's not the size of the dog in the fight, but the size of the fight in the dog." The truth of this axiom is apparent to any sports fan who has seen a larger and stronger opponent vanquished by one who is smaller, weaker, less skilled—but more determined. In war, too, there are innumerable examples of combatants, heavily outnumbered and outgunned, who nonetheless prevailed on the field of battle through sheer will and fighting spirit.

The single most crucial factor in prevailing in a life-threatening encounter is the determination to persevere and win. You must acquire the attitude that if forced to fight, you will never give up.

This attitude of gritty determination is important for several reasons. First, such an attitude, manifested in your speech, eye contact and body language, can throw doubt and fear into a potential assailant, deterring him or her from mounting an attack. If an assault is initiated, sometimes a strong, determined response will cause it to be broken off. Furthermore, even when you are wounded in a confrontation, resolutely continuing your self-defense efforts may stop an attacker before he or she inflicts further injury. There have been many cases of citizens who, though grievously wounded in a criminal attack, refused to give up, and survived their injuries. Finally, your attitude influences your actions. The will to persevere and prevail imbues your efforts with greater power, confidence and effectiveness.

## DEVELOPING A PLAN

An important aspect of mental preparedness and an effective defensive mindset is *planning*. If you are concerned with personal protection, you must develop an individual plan to meet your specific needs. Such a plan should take into consideration your personal characteristics, habits, skills and physical capabilities and limitations, as well as the characteristics of your defensive environment (home or business).

The most important part of any individualized personal protection plan comprises those steps to avoid having to use deadly force. For example, the use of deadlbolt locks, window grills and strategically placed outdoor lighting may help a homeowner avoid using deadly force by deterring a burglar. Alternatively, a planned escape route may allow a store clerk the means to flee an attack without resorting to lethal force. Avoiding a violent confrontation by flight, evasion, deterrence or any other method that can be safely used is always preferable to employing deadly force.

Since the dynamics of any defensive encounter are complex, unpredictable, and changeable, the personal protection plan must offer sufficient flexibility to allow you to make appropriate responses to a wide range of situations. This may involve a series of escalating responses that correspond to different types and levels of threat. Such a series of responses will be discussed in greater detail in Part IV: Strategies for Home and Personal Safety.

Just as you must regularly practice the various shooting and practical skills presented in the NRA Basic Personal Protection in the Home Course to maintain a high level of preparedness, it is also imperative to practice your personal protection plan. Practice your plan using surprise drills, just like you and your family practice the fire evacuation plan you've established for your home. Additionally, frequently review your plan in light of changes in individual characteristics or abilities, the defensive environment, or the nature of the threat(s) likely to be encountered.

# VISUALIZATION

*Visualization* is the formation of a mental image of a situation or activity. Visualization is a powerful tool that has been used to improve performance in sports, business and many other aspects of life.

Visualization should be used to imagine different defensive scenarios in and around the home:

- *What if a strange person suddenly appears at a window?*
- *What if I hear someone attempting to force the lock on my back door?*
- *What if a stranger at my door suddenly produces a knife, club or gun and demands entry into my home?*
- *What if I find my front door unlocked and open when I arrive home?*

Visualizing these and similar scenarios gives you a dry run of such situations, and helps reduce the surprise factor should any of the visualized situations actually take place. Through visualization, you will better anticipate potential sources of danger in the environment, and devise practical plans to deal with them.

Visualization should also be used in one's range training. Visualize the target not as a piece of paper or cardboard, but as a predatory criminal who is threatening your life or the lives of your loved ones. Using this type of imagery during shooting and gun handling exercises will help you mentally prepare for a confrontation with a predatory criminal.

Visualization can additionally be used to build confidence. It has been said that "you can only do what you can see yourself doing." In other words, if you can't picture yourself doing something—whether it is bowling a perfect game, building your own house, or becoming president of a business—you'll probably never be able to do it. Visualization is used this way by many sports psychologists and trainers. They instruct their athletes to visualize themselves not just clearing the hurdles or negotiating the downhill skiing course, but also winning the first place medal. In the same way, when you visualize yourself in a violent encounter, you should complete the mental scenario by visualizing yourself prevailing in that situation. By vividly seeing yourself prevail, and ingraining in yourself the idea that you can and will prevail, you will build confidence in your ability to control a life-threatening situation. That confidence, in turn, will enhance the effectiveness of any defensive actions you take in a real-life confrontation.

## SUMMARY

Shooting, gun handling and practical skills can be critical in helping you prevail in a violent criminal attack, and thus must be diligently practiced. It is equally important, however, to develop and practice the various mental skills, attitudes and techniques—awareness, the willingness to use deadly force, the determination to persevere, planning, and visualization—that together constitute a state of mental preparedness. An individual who possesses only fair marksmanship skills but who has a level of mental preparedness has a greater likelihood of prevailing in a deadly encounter than a highly skilled shooter who lacks the awareness, will to persevere, planning and other factors that contribute to surviving an attack.

# PART III:
# DEVELOPING DEFENSIVE SHOOTING SKILLS

# CHAPTER 6

# DEFENSIVE SHOOTING CONCEPTS

Mental preparedness—being constantly aware of your environment and having a defensive mindset that promotes confidence, perseverance, and planning—often allows you to avoid a violent encounter. However, on occasion it is impossible to sidestep, evade, flee or otherwise escape an attack. At such times your life, and the lives of your loved ones, may depend upon your mastery of defensive shooting skills, such as those presented in the NRA Basic Personal Protection in the Home Course.

Before you can begin to master these skills, however, it is important to understand a number of basic defensive shooting concepts. These concepts underlie both your shooting training and practice as well as any actual deadly force encounter you may face in your home.

## RESPONSIBILITY

Owning a firearm for personal protection is a right that must be exercised responsibly and ethically. Gun owners owe it to themselves, their families and their communities to always use their firearms in a safe and prudent manner.

No matter what the situation, you must always observe the three primary rules of safe gun handling: *ALWAYS* **keep your gun pointed in a safe direction,** *ALWAYS* **keep your finger off the trigger until you are ready to shoot,** and *ALWAYS* **keep your gun unloaded until you are ready to use it.** Being the victim of a violent attack does not permit you to break these rules, or to use your firearm in a way that is hazardous to innocent bystanders.

Responsible behavior entails more than merely adhering to the rules of safe gun handling, however. On some occasions, it may be more responsible not to use your firearm, even when faced with a deadly threat. Often, the determination of what constitutes responsible behavior is a matter of individual judgment.

## IMMINENT DANGER

In most cases, to legally use deadly force, you must be the innocent victim of an attack, and the threat of severe bodily harm must be imminent (about to occur, or immediate). This will be discussed in detail in Part V: Firearms, Self-Defense and the Law.

# TOOL OF LAST RESORT

A firearm is a tool of last resort. It is used only when deadly force is absolutely necessary.

As has been said before, the best way to win a confrontation is to avoid a confrontation. Flight or evasion, if safely possible, is always preferable to the use of lethal force. Legally, in some situations you must do everything in your power to safely flee or evade an encounter before you can resort to your firearm or any other tool of deadly force (see Part V: Firearms, Self-Defense and the Law.) If you employ your firearm against an assailant before you exhaust all possibilities for a non-deadly resolution of the encounter, you not only may be subject to legal sanctions, but also may face the moral condemnation of your family, friends, neighbors, co-workers and others.

# SHOOT TO STOP

The purpose of shooting an assailant is to deprive him of the ability to deliver deadly force. Put another way, you shoot an attacker to cause him to *stop* his life-threatening attack.

Even though a firearm is a tool of deadly or lethal force, your intent when using it against a violent criminal is not to kill, but simply to stop the attack. This is accomplished by shooting at the assailant until he or she is incapacitated or no longer presents a deadly threat. You should stop firing when one or the other of these conditions is met.

Note that you cannot assume your attacker is incapacitated simply because your shots have hit him, even in a vital area. Police reports contain many accounts of felons, high on drugs or possessed of an extreme will to live, who continued their violent depredations even after sustaining lethal wounds to vital areas. You also cannot assume incapacitation just because the assailant has fallen to the ground; he may still be capable of delivering deadly force.

Be aware, too, that a violent criminal may only feign incapacitation to get you to let down your guard. Additionally, a criminal who was genuinely incapacitated at one moment may subsequently (and unexpectedly) revive and again pose a deadly threat.

Sometimes it is not necessary to incapacitate an attacker; he may flee or surrender, no longer presenting a deadly threat. In general, once an attacker no longer presents a threat, you are no longer legally or ethically justified in employing force against that attacker. Consult Part V: Firearms, Self-Defense and the Law, for a more thorough discussion of the limitations on the application of deadly force.

# VIOLENT ENCOUNTERS: CLOSE, QUICK AND DARK

Contrary to what is portrayed in movies and on television, real-life violent encounters occur at very close range, often in reduced-light

conditions, and are over in a matter of seconds. One study of police shootings in a major urban area showed that the majority of encounters took place after dark, at 3 yards or less, in less than 3 seconds, and involved the firing of an average of three shots. This compressed time for most deadly encounters requires an acceleration of many of the fundamentals of handgun shooting.

Furthermore, accounts of defensive and police shootings reveal that it is likely that multiple shots will be required to stop a violent aggressor. Again, the Hollywood depiction of a shooting has little to do with the reality of a

*Fig. 16. This image represents the characteristics of typical violent encounter–it takes place at close range, in the dark, in a brief period of time.*

shooting incident. On television and in the movies, it is easy to see bullet impacts, and a shooting victim is almost invariably downed with a single shot. Often, the person shot is violently thrown backward when hit.

In actuality, it is normally impossible to perceive bullet strikes during a violent confrontation. Things are happening far too quickly, and the target—the violent attacker—is usually moving rapidly, and is in dim light. Often a person does not even show any immediate reaction to being shot, particularly when under the influence of drugs or when in an excited or enraged state. This is why it is important to keep firing at your assailant until he or she no longer presents a deadly threat.

# CENTER OF EXPOSED MASS

Under the conditions of the typical deadly force encounter, you will have to shoot quickly, in low light, at a close, rapidly-moving target. Such

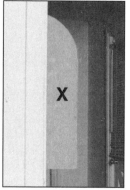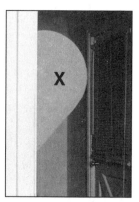

Fig. 17. These photographs demonstrate the "center of exposed mass" aiming point using targets having different degrees of exposure. The "X" marks the center of exposed target mass.

conditions are not conducive to deliberate pinpoint aiming techniques. The defensive aiming technique taught in the NRA Basic Personal Protection in the Home Course is called *center of exposed target mass*. This simply means that you align your sights not on a specific point, but on the approximate center of the target mass that is presented to you. On a standing target out in the open, the center of exposed mass will be located in the middle of the chest. In other cases, such as when an attacker is partially behind cover, the center of exposed mass may be located elsewhere.

# DEFENSIVE ACCURACY

Closely related to the use of a center of exposed mass aiming area is the concept of defensive accuracy. While the ability of both gun and shooter to group shots tightly is critical in the various handgun sports, the characteristics of most defensive encounters make the attainment of pinpoint accuracy both unrealistic and unnecessary. As noted above, defensive shootings generally take place at close range (less than 7 yards) and in dim light, and are concluded in only a few seconds. Often, either the assailant or the defender — or both — are moving rapidly during the encounter. Such conditions do not permit the careful alignment of the sights on a specific aiming point on the target.

Simply put, defensive accuracy is that level of accuracy that allows the shooter to keep all shots in an assailant's vital area. If a center-of-mass hold is used on a fully exposed target, this area is equal to approximately a 9-inch circle — about the size of an average paper plate or sheet of standard typing paper. This minimum level of accuracy (all shots on an 8½ inch by

The Basics of Personal Protection in the Home

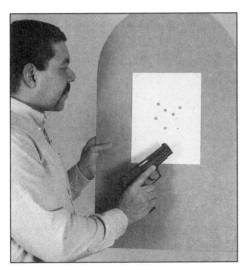

*Fig.18. This grouping on an 8½" by 11" piece of paper represents adequate defensive accuracy.*

11 inch sheet of paper at 7 yards) is well within the capabilities of virtually any shooter with a quality handgun.

This discussion of defensive accuracy should not be construed to minimize the importance of accuracy in a defensive shooting situation. Virtually all self-defense authorities agree that accurate shot placement is the key to quickly stopping an aggressive attack. The accuracy standard stated above should be regarded as the minimum level of accuracy that is acceptable for defensive purposes. The responsible defensive-minded shooter will endeavor to exceed this standard. In any defensive shooting situation, the more accurate the shooter/handgun combination, the greater the likelihood that the aggressor will be quickly incapacitated.

# CHAPTER 7

# BASIC DEFENSIVE SHOOTING SKILLS

Like other forms of handgun shooting, defensive shooting is based upon the fundamental principles of pistol marksmanship. These fundamentals are aiming, breath control, hold control, trigger control and follow-through. The special dynamics of aggressive encounters require you to apply these fundamentals in a manner that is more accelerated than when you are target shooting or plinking.

## FIREARM SAFETY

The most basic of all shooting principles deal with gun safety. Whether practicing at the range, cleaning your gun in your workshop, or retrieving your gun from its storage location in your home, the fundamental rules of safe gun handling still apply: **ALWAYS keep the gun pointed in a safe direction**; **ALWAYS keep your finger off the trigger until ready to shoot**; and **ALWAYS keep the gun unloaded until ready to use**.

In the overwhelming stress and confusion of a defensive encounter, it is easy to forget or disregard even the most basic of gun safety rules. Through constant repetition and mindfulness, however, the basic gun safety rules can become gun safety habits that function even during a violent confrontation.

## AIMING

*Aiming* is the process of aligning a firearm with a target so that a bullet fired from that firearm will strike the target where desired. In other words, the point of aim will coincide with the point of impact. Aiming is normally accomplished using the gun's sights. Most sights on defensive handguns take the form of a flat-topped front post and a square-cornered rear notch.

Aiming consists of two stages: sight alignment and sight picture. *Sight alignment* refers to the proper positioning of the shooting eye, the rear sight, and the front sight in relation to each other. With the notch-and-post system typically found on defensive firearms, the proper sight alignment for precise shooting occurs when the front post is centered laterally (same amount of space on either side of the front post) in the rear notch, and the tops of both the post and the notch line up. Visual focus is on the front sight. For defensive shooting purposes at close range (3 to 7 yards), however, it is usually sufficient to simply place the front sight post somewhere inside the rear sight notch. This gives an allowable sight deviation that will still keep your shots within the critical aiming area—roughly equivalent to an 8½ inch by 11 inch sheet of paper—at up to about 9 yards, depending upon your gun's sights. Just as in the precision sight alignment used for slower shooting, the visual focus in the sight alignment method used in defensive situations is still on the front sight.

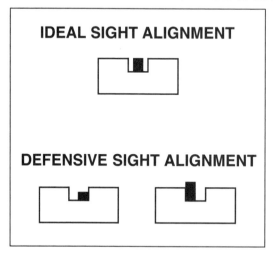

**IDEAL SIGHT ALIGNMENT**

**DEFENSIVE SIGHT ALIGNMENT**

*Fig. 19. In ideal sight alignment, the front post is centered in the rear notch, and the tops of both sights are exactly even. In defensive sight alignment, you may fire whenever the post is visible somewhere in the notch.*

*Sight picture* refers to the relationship between the gun's properly aligned sights and the target. For the purposes of effective defensive shooting, the handgun's aligned sights are placed on the center of exposed mass of the target. That is, the sights are placed in the middle of the target area that is exposed or selected.

During an emergency defensive response, your trigger finger should start in motion automatically when your eye sees that the sights are aligned on the center of target mass. The use of a larger aiming area (the center of target mass) instead of a small exact aiming point on the target allows you to develop this automatic response to an acceptable sight picture. A larger aiming area also helps you stay focused on the front sight and permits smooth trigger control.

# BREATH CONTROL

*Breath control* is the method used to minimize gun movement due to breathing. With each breath, your ribcage expands and your shoulders rise slightly. This movement is transmitted to your arms, causing your aimed handgun to shift position in relation to the target.

Although target competitors and other precision handgun shooters practice sophisticated breath control methods to minimize gun movement, these methods generally are not applicable in a defensive confrontation. In such a situation, fear for your life, trying to evade or escape an attack, and attempting to scream a warning to your attacker can all leave you gasping for breath. Your heart will be pounding and your lungs will be demanding air. Breath control under these circumstances involves simply stopping breathing and holding it. Breathing should simply cease momentarily while the shot is being fired. This will steady the position and allow for a quick shot or series of shots. While this method works only for a few seconds, it should be sufficient for the duration of a typical armed response to an attack. In some cases, in fact, the armed defender may have to make a conscious effort to resume breathing after shooting has ended.

## HOLD CONTROL

Maximum accuracy is achieved when the firearm is held motionless during the process of aiming and firing. *Hold control* is the method by which both the body and the gun are held as still as possible while the shot is fired.

The armed citizen acting in self-defense does not have this luxury. In a defensive shooting situation, hold control is achieved primarily through a well-balanced, stable shooting position that is naturally aligned with the target. More information on these positions and on target alignment is found in Chapter 8: Shooting Positions.

## TRIGGER CONTROL

*Trigger control* is one of the most important of shooting fundamentals. The term refers to the technique of releasing the trigger without causing any movement of the sights.

In most basic firearm training courses, beginning shooters are taught to

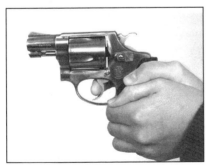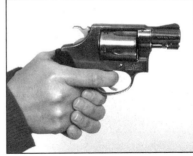

*Fig. 20. Proper defensive shooting trigger finger placement on a revolver, seen from both sides.*

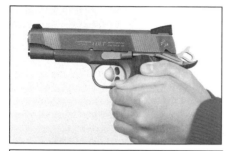

Fig. 21. Proper defensive shooting trigger finger placement on a semi-automatic pistol, seen from the left (top) and the right.

apply gradually increasing pressure to the trigger so that it breaks in a surprise manner. The brief duration of a defensive encounter makes a slow, gradual trigger squeeze impractical, however. Nonetheless, trigger control is still critical; poor trigger technique can easily cause a shooter to completely miss even a large target at close range.

Trigger control in a defensive shooting environment involves speeding up the process of squeezing the trigger without jerking or flinching. The more smoothly the shooter pulls the trigger, the less the gun's sights will be disturbed during the firing process, even when the time period of the pull is compressed for faster shooting.

Good trigger control also involves the proper placement of the trigger finger on the trigger. A properly placed trigger finger allows the force of the pull to be directed straight to the rear, minimizing a tendency to jerk the gun to the right or left. Proper placement also allows the gun to be fired by moving only the trigger finger.

For single-action shooting, the trigger should be pulled using the middle of the last pad of the trigger finger. For double-action shooting, the trigger should be placed approximately on the joint between the last and middle pads of the

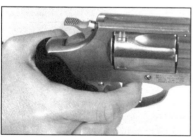

Fig. 22. Photos showing the proper gap between the trigger finger and the frame of a revolver (left) and a semi-automatic pistol.

The Basics of Personal Protection in the Home

trigger finger. The ideal trigger finger placement can be achieved through dry-fire practice at a sheet of white paper. Adjust your finger position until there is no movement in sight alignment when the trigger is pulled and the hammer or striker falls. Note that the proper contact point on the trigger finger may change from gun to gun and firing position to firing position.

If possible, you should also leave a small gap between your trigger finger and the frame of the handgun to prevent the finger from contacting or dragging on the frame and thus disturbing sight alignment as the trigger is pulled.

# FOLLOW-THROUGH

The concept of *follow-though* is common to many sports, such as golf, tennis, baseball, bowling and archery. In shooting, follow-through is the effort made by the shooter to integrate, maintain and continue all shooting fundamentals before, during and immediately after the firing of the shot.

It is true that any alteration in the gun position, stance, sight alignment, and so forth that occurs after the bullet has left the muzzle has no effect whatsoever on accuracy or shot placement. Nonetheless, it is important to consciously maintain the shooting fundamentals for a brief time after the shot has been fired because only by doing so will you be certain that

*Fig. 23. Proper follow-through allows this shooter to fire two accurate shots in rapid succession. The white arrow indicates the fired case from the first shot; the black arrow indicates the case from the second shot, just leaving the pistol.*

those fundamentals are applied before and during the firing of the shot. Thus, proper follow-through minimizes gun movement as the shot is fired. A shooter who fails to follow through and applies the fundamentals only up to the breaking of the trigger will (in anticipation of the shot) inevitably abandon one or more of the fundamentals just prior to firing, resulting in errant bullet flight.

Proper follow-through does more than just ensure adherence to the shooting fundamentals through the firing of the shot. Follow-through also sets up any successive shots that may be necessary. As mentioned above, in defensive encounters it is likely that you will have to fire multiple shots to quickly stop an assailant. By following through, you can maintain your stance, alignment with the target, and sight alignment, allowing easy recovery of the proper sight picture and the fastest possible follow-up shot. During the follow-through period, you also relax trigger finger pressure, allowing the trigger to reset, but still maintain finger contact with the trigger face.

The follow-through used in defensive shooting is highly compressed to last only a fraction of a second. You can also use this period of time to recover the sights after the shot, assess the effects of the shots fired, and prepare for additional shots if necessary.

## SUMMARY

All of the basic defensive shooting skills are integrated in the firing of a shot in self defense. The shooter aims (maintaining both sight alignment and a center-of-mass sight picture) while momentarily stopping respiration (breath control) and movement (hold control). Only the trigger finger, properly placed, is moved to fire the shot (trigger control). Before, during and after the shot is fired, the shooter observes all the proper shooting fundamentals, and recovers the sights and aligns them back onto the target immediately after firing the shot (follow-through).

# CHAPTER 8

# SHOOTING POSITIONS

As presented in the previous chapter, the fundamental principles of handgun marksmanship are still observed in a defensive shooting situation, albeit in a modified manner. Effective shooting takes more than just adherence to these fundamentals, however. An effective shooting position is the platform from which the fundamentals are applied.

## ELEMENTS OF A SHOOTING POSITION

Although there are many effective shooting positions for many different situations, all share a number of common characteristics: *consistency, balance, support, natural aiming area* and *comfort.*

*Consistency* is critical because variations in position produce variations in impact point and/or group size. You must strive to assume each position in the same exact way every time. In the training phase, this is accomplished by conscious attention to each aspect of the position and each step taken to assume it. With repetition, this process of developing a position "by the numbers" will become ingrained in your subconscious mind, eventually enabling you to flow into the position quickly, effortlessly, naturally and consistently. The "muscle memory" thus developed through rigorous practice will allow the position to be assumed automatically in an emergency situation.

*Balance* is also an essential component of a proper firing position. Balance is usually best achieved in a stance with the feet spaced at shoulders-width, even weight distribution, and a slightly forward, aggressive lean with the majority of the weight on the balls of the feet.

A position that is balanced provides the most stable shooting platform, one that absorbs recoil and facilitates both movement and accurate follow-up shots. A balanced position with the head upright and level also is important for controlling body movement. The brain senses body position by a number of mechanisms, including a structure in the inner ear known as the *labyrinthe.* An upright, level head position will

*Fig. 24. A balanced shooting position.*

43

maximize the ability of the labyrinthe to promote body equilibrium and efficient body movement.

A good position also offers *support* to minimize gun movement while aiming. Support can be provided by the skeleton, muscle tension or an external object, such as a table or trash can providing cover or concealment. A two-handed grip, for example, efficiently uses muscle tension to provide more support than a one-handed grip. Generally, standing positions offer less support than kneeling and prone positions. Even the support offered by one-handed positions can be maximized, however, by ensuring that the stance is balanced, the grip is firm, and the shooter is properly aligned with the target.

*Fig 25. A good shooting position offers support. The shooter above makes use of skeletal support by bracing her support arm on the knee. The position of the left foot directly below the knee relieves the leg muscles of any support role; support is provided only by the rigid bones of the lower leg, ankle and foot. At left, the shooter uses the object providing cover or concealment to support her shooting position. Note that her arms, and not the pistol, rest on the supporting object.*

All effective firing positions incorporate the shooter's *natural aiming area (NAA)*. NAA refers to the individual, instinctive alignment of the shooter and the gun in a specific stance, when that stance feels most balanced and comfortable to the shooter. To determine your NAA in a particular stance, you should first assume that stance, with your eyes open and your gun aimed at a target at a moderate distance. Next, close your eyes. With your eyes still closed, settle into the position that feels most stable and comfortable, and take several breaths. Then, open your eyes and observe where your gun's sights are pointed in relation to the target. The

The Basics of Personal Protection in the Home

*Fig. 26. In the NAA (Natural Aiming Area) exercise, the shooter (A) first assumes a stance with the gun aimed at a target at moderate distance. Then (B) the eyes are closed, and (C) the shooter settles into the shooting position that feels most comfortable and stable. Note the shift of the gun position from (B) to (C). When the shooter's eyes open (D) and she observes where the gun's sights are pointed in relation to the target, her foot position or some other aspect of her stance can be modified to achieve the proper sight picture while taking full advantage of her body's natural aiming area.*

sights will often be aligned to the right or left or slightly high or low, requiring you to modify your foot position or some other aspect of your stance to achieve the proper sight picture while taking full advantage of your body's NAA.

Repeat the NAA exercise until your stance is adjusted for the proper natural alignment. You should make every effort to adopt this same alignment each time the stance is assumed in order to take advantage of your NAA.

Finally, a proper stance should be *comfortable*. A stance that is not comfortable—one that is forced, awkward, strained or painful—is unlikely to be consistent or stable, and thus will not contribute to effective shooting. When practicing shooting positions, you should be conscious of how natural and comfortable each position is. Positions that do not feel comfortable must be modified as necessary. However, in some cases discomfort may be the result of the lack of joint flexibility or muscular strength. In such cases, a minimal amount of physical training is usually all that is needed to allow the shooter to comfortably assume a proper shooting stance.

# THE TWO-HANDED GRIP

Under most conditions, you will grip the handgun with a two-handed grip. For the vast majority of shooters, such a grip provides more control of the firearm, better recoil absorption, steadier aiming and stronger gun retention.

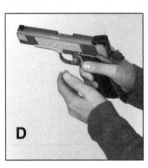

To assume the grip, first grasp the handgun in your weak (non-firing) hand. Make a "Y" of the thumb and fingers of the strong (firing) hand (A), and place the gun's backstrap firmly in the web of the thumb (B). Then wrap the fingers of the strong hand around the handgun's grip (C).

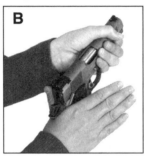

*Fig. 27. The steps in assuming a proper two-handed grip on a handgun. Letters refer to steps described in text.*

Next, bring the weak hand around the front of the grip (D) so that the weak hand fingers overlie and overlap the strong hand fingers (E). The first joint of the weak hand fingers should be approximately aligned with the knuckles of the

The Basics of Personal Protection in the Home

strong hand, and the weak hand thumb will lie directly forward of and below the strong hand thumb (F). Gripping the firearm with tension from both the weak and strong hands creates a steadier hold on the pistol, and makes it extremely difficult for an attacker to take it away from you.

Grip consistency is essential for accurate shooting, whether in bullseye competition or in a defensive encounter. Use dry-fire practice to check and reinforce the correct trigger finger placement (see Chapter 12: Opportunities for Skills Enhancement). Note that the proper grip for one specific firearm may not be appropriate for another firearm; your grip may vary depending upon the angle, thickness, shape and length of a gun's grip frame. Also, your grip may vary slightly from position to position.

# READY POSITIONS

In many defensive situations, such as when you are in your safe room listening for the approach of an intruder, you will not immediately go into a firing position. Often, you will hold your firearm in a ready position for extended periods of time, in anticipation of use. Two ready positions are presented in this course: the *low ready position* and the *retention ready position*.

*Fig. 28. The low ready position.*

**Low Ready Position.** To assume the low ready position, take the proper grip on the handgun and extend the arms outward and downward at approximately a 45-degree angle. The firearm will be oriented toward a point on the ground several feet in front of you. Your knees should be slightly bent and the weight slightly forward, in anticipation of either movement or the sudden acquisition of a full firing position. Your foot and shoulder position should reflect the firing stance that you plan to assume (e.g., isosceles, Weaver, etc.).

Another way of visualizing the low ready position is to adopt the shooting stance and then simply lower the extended arms to approximately a 45-degree downward angle.

The simplicity of the low ready position is one of its primary advantages. Another benefit of the stance is that it permits easy assumption of the full shooting position. Since the arms are already extended, the wrists are already locked and the feet and shoulders already aligned, it is simply a matter of raising the gun to eye level to acquire the sights and shoot.

The primary limitation to the low ready position is that it puts your firearm well out away from your body, making it possible, at close quarters, for an adversary to block the rise of the gun to a firing position. Even worse, it may enable an attacker to grab and wrest your firearm from you.

**Retention Ready Position.** The retention ready position gets its name from the way it places the firearm close to the body, almost tucked into the armpit. The retention position can be visualized by assuming the normal shooting position and then simply pulling the firearm to the rear, into the body directly in front of the strong-side armpit. The two-handed grip is retained, and the firearm is pointed forward, toward the target with the barrel parallel to the ground.

*Fig. 29. The retention ready position.*

The retention ready position has several advantages. First, by keeping the handgun close to the body, it promotes gun retention and hinders an attacker's efforts to block or grab it. You can easily go from the retention position to the full shooting position by simply extending the arms forward. Additionally, since your firearm is kept pointed at the target in the retention position, a shot may actually be fired from the position if necessary (for example, if an attacker lunges at you at arm's length).

Do not raise the muzzle of your gun or point it upward as it is brought in toward the body. Not only does this negate the advantages that accrue from keeping the firearm pointed at the target, but a muzzle-upward orientation can actually be hazardous if you are suddenly startled and reflexively fire the

The Basics of Personal Protection in the Home

firearm. Aside from the potential for facial powder burns and possible eye damage, a shot fired under such circumstances can result in a wayward bullet that could penetrate a ceiling to injure someone in the floor above.

# TWO-HANDED SHOOTING POSITIONS

Two basic shooting positions are taught in this course: the *Isosceles position* and the *Weaver position*. In addition, a modified version of each basic position is also presented.

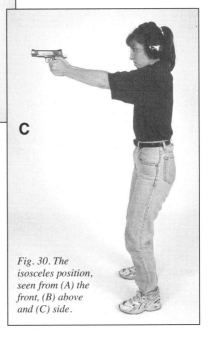

**Isosceles Position.** The Isosceles position is so named because in this position your extended arms, when seen from above, resemble an isosceles triangle. In the isosceles stance, your feet are placed at about shoulder width, and your feet and shoulders are square with the target. Your knees are slightly bent and your weight is slightly forward, on the balls of the feet. The pistol is grasped in a normal two-handed grip, and is held with both your arms extended fully forward. Your elbows are straight but not locked. Your head is erect, not hunched; your shoulders are at their normal height, not raised; and your firearm is lifted to the level of your eyes for aiming.

The isosceles position is a very natural shooting position. Under the stress of an actual defensive shooting situation, many shooters instinctively adopt a modified "instinctive" form of this position. The ease with which you can pivot laterally in the isosceles stance

*Fig. 30. The isosceles position, seen from (A) the front, (B) above and (C) side.*

facilitates the engagement of multiple targets. The primary limitation of the stance is that, at very close range, the arm's length position of the gun may facilitate an attacker's block or grab.

*Fig. 31. The Weaver position from the front.*

**Weaver Position.** The Weaver position is named for former Los Angeles County Sheriff Jack Weaver, who is credited with originating it in the 1950s. To assume the Weaver position, place your body in a rough boxer's stance with your strong hand foot rearward, your weak side shoulder angled toward the target, your knees slightly flexed and your body weight carried slightly forward, on the balls of your feet. Grasp your gun in a normal two-handed grip, but bend both elbows (the weak- or support-hand elbow pointing downward) to bring the handgun closer to the body than in the isosceles stance. The location of the handgun often requires that your head tip slightly to properly view the sights. Tension between the two hands is perhaps the most functionally significant feature of this position: the strong hand is pushed forward into the weak hand, which simultaneously pulls rearward. This push-pull tension creates great stability and steadiness.

The Weaver position gives considerable support to the firearm, and by pulling the gun in closer to the body, affords better gun retention and better maneuverability in tight quarters. Also, the bent elbows and asymmetrical foot position enhance recoil absorption. When a shot is fired, the bent elbows act as springs, bending to absorb recoil forces and then returning the gun to its original position. With heavy-recoiling handguns, the Weaver position affords fast shot-to-shot recovery for many shooters.

**Modified Isosceles Position.** This position incorporates the natural, fully-extended arm position of the isosceles position with the stability of the asymmetrical boxer's stance foot placement of the Weaver position, which allows better recoil absorption. The head is level and the body leans forward. Often the shoulders rise reflexively, resulting in the instinctive stance referred to above. The modified isosceles position also represents the stance that would result when a shooter in the standard isosceles position pivots sharply to the side.

**Modified Weaver Position.** The modified Weaver position is very similar to the standard Weaver stance, with the exception that your strong-side arm is almost completely extended toward the target. Your weak-side arm is still bent, however, and your weak hand still pulls rearward against the forward-pushing strong hand. It is important to note that your strong-side arm is not locked but slightly bent, enabling it to flex and absorb recoil. For many shooters, the modified Weaver position offers the same stability as the standard Weaver position, but feels more

*Fig. 32. The modified Weaver position.*

natural. Some shooters in this position may have to tilt the head slightly to see the gun's sights, but for many the modified Weaver position allows a more upright and level head position than the standard Weaver position.

# ONE-HANDED SHOOTING POSITIONS

The well-rounded defensive shooter must be as comfortable with one-handed firing positions as with the more familiar two-handed ones. There are many situations in which one-handed firing may be necessary. For example, an injury to a hand or arm might make a two-hand hold impossible to assume. Alternatively, it may be necessary to use one hand to ward off blows or the thrusts of a knife, hold a flashlight or telephone, retrieve a dropped magazine or revolver speedloader, feel for obstructions in a darkened room, shield a child, and so forth.

The one-handed shooting positions used in defensive situations—the *reverse punch* and *forward punch* positions—are similar to stances used in the martial arts.

**Reverse Punch Position.** In this position, you assume a boxer's stance,

Fig. 33. The reverse punch position.

with your foot on the weak-hand (non-firing) side forward, your strong-side foot back, and your upper body bladed away from the target (that is, your upper body does not directly face the target, but is angled away so that your strong-side shoulder is somewhat to the rear). Your non-firing arm is drawn in toward the middle of the chest to keep it out of the way of the muzzle, and your non-firing hand is held palm-out to ward off an attacker. With your hand in this palm-out position, you can push an attacker away with the powerful triceps muscle of your upper arm.

Your firing arm is bent slightly at the elbow, and your firing hand is canted inward at a natural angle—the same natural angle created when you form a fist in this position. [Note that, under most firing conditions, canting the firearm is detrimental to accuracy, and thus is generally discouraged. However, at the short distances typical of a violent attack, canting has little detrimental effect.] Your upper body leans slightly forward, with most of your body weight on your forward (weak-side) leg. Your strong-side leg acts as a brace to support an aggressive, forward-leaning stance, with your weight carried on the ball of your strong-side foot.

The reverse-punch position can be easily assumed from the retention ready position, simply by pushing the gun forward. When practicing this position, be careful to keep the weak hand drawn in toward the middle of the chest, clear of the muzzle. If the handgun is discharged while in the ready position and the forward, weak hand is not clear of the muzzle, a wound to the hand or arm will result. Note that it may not always be possible, when struggling with an

Fig. 34. The forward punch position.

The Basics of Personal Protection in the Home

attacker, to keep the weak hand clear of the muzzle. In a life-or-death situation, however, it may be necessary to risk a self-inflicted injury to protect your life or the lives of your loved ones.

The reverse punch position is particularly suited for close-quarters confrontations, as it puts the defensive hand forward to more effectively ward off an assailant, and positions the gun closer to the body, promoting gun retention.

**Forward Punch Position.** The forward punch position is similar to the reverse punch position, except that the foot, hand and shoulder on the strong (firing) side are now forward, leading toward the target. Your body still assumes a forward-leaning stance, and your weak hand is still drawn in toward the middle of your chest, in a defensive, palm-out position. Aside from the defensive position of the non-firing hand and the aggressive body position, there is a degree of similarity between the forward punch position and the one-handed stance used by bullseye shooters.

# KNEELING POSITIONS

To take advantage of cover and concealment (see Chapter 10: Utilizing Cover and Concealment) it may be necessary to adopt firing positions other than the standing positions previously presented. The kneeling positions presented in this handbook—the *high kneeling*, *low kneeling*, *supported kneeling* and *double kneeling* positions—allow the shooter to take advantage of low cover or concealment, such as a bed, chair, fence or trash can.

Kneeling positions have other advantages, too. Even where there is no cover or concealment, a kneeling position makes you a smaller target, reducing the likelihood of being hit by hostile fire. Kneeling positions are also generally more stable than standing positions, thus enhancing shooting accuracy.

A kneeling firing position may also allow you to remain undetected by an assailant and thus avoid confrontation altogether, or, if necessary, to take that assailant by surprise. An attacker who expects to see his or her victim at normal standing eye level may be unprepared to respond quickly to a defender below normal eye level. In fact, a defender effectively using low cover or concealment in a kneeling position may not even be seen by an aggressor, especially under low-light conditions.

For most shooters, kneeling positions are quick to move into and out of, and thus are frequently used in defensive shooting situations. The serious defensive shooter should practice the various kneeling positions until they are achieved easily and naturally.

**High Kneeling Position.** In the high kneeling position, the upper body

*Fig. 35. The high kneeling position.*

position is essentially the same as that of a standing two-handed position, the weak-side leg is bent and serves as the support leg, and the strong-side knee is placed on the ground. The body leans slightly forward to counter recoil. For maximum stability, it is important that the strong-side foot rests on the toes and forward part of the ball of the foot, the line between the knee and hip of the strong-side leg is vertical (perpendicular to the ground), and the support-leg knee is directly over the toe. These specific foot and leg placements are essential to ensure that the position is balanced and stable, and to allow you to efficiently move into and out of the position as necessary.

It is also important to keep your strong-side lower leg directly behind your thigh. Many shooters are tempted to move the strong-side foot inward until it is in line with the support-leg foot, to gain extra stability. Although this position is indeed more solid, it rotates the strong-side thigh outward, exposing the femoral artery to incoming fire.

The high kneeling position may be assumed in two ways; in either method, the pistol must point in a safe direction at all times and not cross, or point at, any part of your body. First, you may step forward with your support leg at the same time your strong-side knee is lowered to the ground. In this technique, the strong-side foot remains in place. Alternatively, you may step back with your strong-side foot and then drop your strong-side knee straight down into position. The former procedure may be used when you are approaching cover, or where there is sufficient space to allow the forward step. When you are already close to the object providing cover, or wish to distance yourself from it, the second kneeling technique is used.

While assuming a high kneeling position using either technique, the muzzle must be kept pointing in a safe direction. If you go into a kneeling position from a ready position, a retention ready position is preferable to a low ready position. For many shooters, the retention ready position provides better balance while dropping into a kneeling position, and keeps

The Basics of Personal Protection in the Home

*Fig. 36. This sequence shows the assumption of the high kneeling position. From the low ready position (A), the shooter steps back with the strong-side foot (B) and extends the gun toward the target (C). The shooter then drops straight down onto the strong-side knee (D), making sure that the weak-side knee is directly above the foot. Finally, the shooter leans toward the target slightly to provide better balance and to counteract recoil (E).*

the muzzle pointing toward the target rather than downward at the support leg or foot, or the object providing cover. Your arms are extended forward into a firing position as your knee contacts the ground.

**Low Kneeling Position.** The low kneeling position allows both a lower shooter position as well as greater stability than the high kneeling position. In terms of leg position it is essentially identical to the high kneeling position, with the exception that the strong-side foot may rest on the ball of the foot or may be placed flat along the ground, for a lower profile. The upper body position differs considerably, however. Instead of the relatively erect posture of the

*Fig. 37. The low kneeling position. Note the effective support for the non-dominant hand.*

high kneeling position, the body is bent forward until the support-side arm rests on the knee of the support leg, with the contact point of the arm located above the elbow. The greater degree of forward lean results in both a lower position as well as better recoil absorption.

The increased stability of the low kneeling position results from both its

*Fig. 38. Two versions of the low kneeling position, as seen from the rear. The difference is primarily in the position of the strong-side foot. In one version the strong-side foot contacts the ground on the ball of the foot (A). Alternatively, the foot can be placed flat on the ground under the body (B). The latter position allows a slightly lower profile and may be more comfortable for some shooters.*

The Basics of Personal Protection in the Home

lower shooter posture as well as its effective use of bone structure to provide support. It is therefore a particularly good position when great accuracy is required. However, it is slower to get into and out of than the high kneeling position. The low kneeling position can be assumed either by stepping forward with the support leg or stepping rearward with the strong-side leg.

The low kneeling position is preferred when cover is low, when increased stability is needed to hit a smaller target, or when there is sufficient time to assume the position. Even when cover is sufficiently high to justify a high kneeling position, a low kneeling position may expose less of your body to an attacker, and its recoil-absorbing qualities may allow you faster follow-up shots.

**Supported Kneeling Position.** In the supported kneeling position, the handgun is supported on the object providing cover or concealment, such as a mattress, trash can lid, countertop or file cabinet. In this position, your lower-body positioning is similar to that used in the high kneeling and low kneeling positions. Your upper body leans forward, both to absorb recoil and to enable you to get as low as possible.

Note that only your hands, wrists or arms, and not the handgun itself, make direct contact with the object providing cover or concealment. A handgun that is fired when its grip is resting on a solid surface likely will place its shots in a different location than when fired from an unsupported or *offhand* position, and may also produce larger groups. Furthermore, supporting some semi-automatic pistols on their magazine baseplates makes them more prone to malfunction. In addition, allowing your handgun to contact a hard object may produce a telltale sound that gives away your position or spoils the element of surprise.

*Fig. 39. The supported kneeling position. Note that the shooter's arms, and not the handgun itself, contact the support object, and that the shooter has achieved a balanced position by sitting back on her heels.*

If the supporting object is very low, it is preferable to sit back into the position slightly rather than bend too far forward at the waist. By sitting back, the weight of your upper body is still centered over your lower body, giving better balance and allowing rapid movement if necessary. Excessively bending the upper body forward shifts your balance too far to

*Fig. 40. The low (left) and high double kneeling positions.*

the front to allow quick changes in position.

**Double Kneeling Position.** The double kneeling position is probably the quickest of all the kneeling positions to get into. Simply bend both knees simultaneously, dropping them to the ground. Your body leans slightly forward to absorb recoil and the line between your hip and knee is not perpendicular to the ground but angled slightly to the rear, for better balance. The lower your position, the more you will have to sit back in the position to keep the body weight centered.

While the double kneeling position is fast and simple to assume, it may not be appropriate for older, less flexible shooters, or those with knee problems. Also, there is a possibility of knee injury if the knees are driven hard into an unyielding concrete or asphalt surface. In addition, for heavier or older shooters, the double kneeling position may present more of a challenge to move from.

# SQUATTING POSITION

In some situations it may be necessary to quickly minimize exposure to an adversary, but it may not be possible or desirable to assume a kneeling position. This might be the case when the surface underfoot is uneven, strewn with broken glass, poorly seen (as in very low light) or likely to make a telltale sound that would give away your position. Under these conditions, you can simply squat straight down behind cover or concealment.

*Fig. 41. The squatting shooting position is perhaps the quickest position to assume from a standing position, and is achieved by simply squatting straight down.*

The primary advantages of the squatting position are simplicity, quickness and silence. Some shooters may have difficulty maintaining balance while in this position; stability may be improved by widening the stance and placing the strong-side foot slightly to the rear of the weak-side foot. Additional stability may be acquired by supporting the extended arms on the object providing cover or concealment. Even with such support, the squatting position is not as stable as any of the kneeling positions. Also, older persons or those with knee problems or weak leg muscles may find the squatting position taxing to maintain or move from. Even young and fit persons will likely experience leg muscle tremor after a minute or so in this position; the squatting position should thus be considered a temporary position.

# CHAPTER 9

# AIMING AND FIRING TECHNIQUES

Mastering the fundamentals of handgun shooting and the various defensive shooting positions only partially prepares you to use a handgun effectively to protect your life. It is also essential to understand and apply other defense-related skills and concepts, such as defensive accuracy, flash sight picture, point shooting, firing multiple shots, engaging multiple assailants, and breaking tunnel vision to assess for additional threats.

## DEFENSIVE ACCURACY

Violent encounters typically take place at a distance of only a few feet and are completed in a few seconds, and the target area (the vital area of an assailant) is fairly large. Thus, a high level of pinpoint accuracy is not required of the shooter, the gun or the ammunition. A good general estimate is that the ability to keep all shots on a standard 8½ inch by 11 inch sheet of paper at 7 yards, hitting in the center of exposed mass, is sufficient for most defensive purposes.

Experienced shooters will recognize that this is an extremely modest level of accuracy, well within the capabilities of virtually any handgun even in only moderately skilled hands. However, what can be easily attained in a well-lit practice range, firing at a stationary target using a stable two-hand hold, is far different than what can be expected during the stress of being suddenly attacked by a violent, hostile, rapidly-moving person in a low-light situation.

Fig. 42. Adequate defensive accuracy as reflected by this group fired on an 8½" by 11" sheet of paper at seven yards.

In the vast majority of defensive encounters, it is essential to fire as fast as you accurately can. Both a proper shooting position and good execution of the shooting fundamentals are essential to accurate, rapid fire.

Inevitably, there will be a certain degree of shot dispersion around the center of mass. This is not the result of deliberately aiming at different spots. All shots are aimed at the same area—the center of exposed mass.

61

The shots are spread out due to the speed with which shots are fired and the less-than-perfect alignment of the sights.

Note that if you are shooting ragged one-hole groups in the center of the exposed target mass during practice, you should probably be shooting faster. If your shots are spreading to the edge of a large target, beyond the

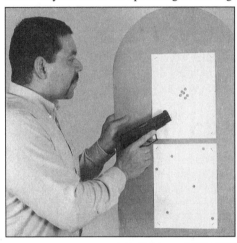

maximum allowable group size (an 8½ inch by 11 inch sheet of paper) at 7 yards, you should slow down. Also, while the old adages "a slow hit beats a fast miss" and "you can't miss fast enough" are certainly true, there is such a thing as taking too much time to fire the shot.

Probably more than any other factor, the effects of stress are responsible for the deterioration in accuracy often observed during defensive shooting situations. Studies of shooting incidents involving law enforcement officers, which typically take place at relatively close range, show that police officers achieve hits less than 20 percent of the time. In other words, four out of five shots fired by trained law enforcement officers miss the target completely. Even under the

*Fig. 43. If you are shooting tight seven-yard groups, as in the upper target (above), you should speed up your shooting. If some of the shots in your group are almost off the paper, slow down. The group shown at right represents good accuracy for defensive purposes.*

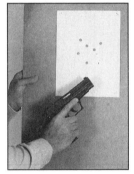

relatively modest level of stress imposed by activities such as practical shooting competition, it is not uncommon for shooters to completely miss a large, close target.

Poor shooting is not inevitable under the extreme stress of a defensive encounter, however. Your actual shooting performance during such an encounter can be improved by incorporating stress and realism in your training regimen, and by always striving for a higher level of accuracy. A shooter who can keep his or her shots within 3 inches at 7 yards has much more of a margin for stress-induced error than one who can do no better than 8 inches at the same distance.

The Basics of Personal Protection in the Home

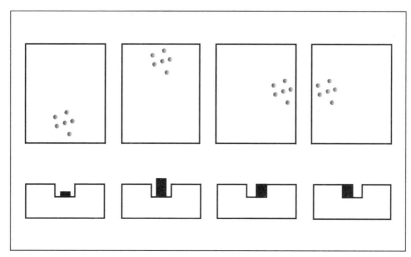

*Fig. 44. Acceptable defensive or "flash" sight pictures, with the expected placement of the group on an 8½" x 11" sheet of paper at 7 yards in relation to a central aiming point.*

## FLASH SIGHT PICTURE

From the foregoing discussion of defensive accuracy, it is clearly neither necessary nor desirable for you to strive for pinpoint precision accuracy in a defensive shooting situation. The large size of the target and the close range involved usually allows you to have a shot dispersion, or group size, of several inches and still remain in the vital area. More importantly, the extremely rapid nature of most violent attacks requires you to get hits on an assailant as quickly as possible. Usually you cannot afford the time it takes to precisely align the front sight post in the rear notch.

The aiming technique most often used to produce quick yet acceptably accurate hits with a defensive handgun is known as *flash sight picture*. In this technique, the shot is fired as soon as the front sight is roughly lined up somewhere within the rear sight notch. The front sight blade may be slightly off to the right or left, or may be slightly high or low. As long as it is visible somewhere in the rear sight notch, your shots will fall within an 8½ inch by 11 inch piece of paper at 7 yards.

For those using very short-barreled handguns, the precision of sight alignment—even with a flash sight picture—is more critical than for longer-barreled models. This is because the closer the front and rear sights are, the greater the inaccuracy resulting from any misalignment of the sights.

A flash sight picture is used for the first shot fired at an attacker when that shot is delivered at close range, and must be taken quickly. The technique is also used to deliver rapid follow-up shots, or to quickly engage several threats at the same time.

With practice, it will become possible for you to acquire a flash sight picture within a fraction of a second of bringing the sights onto the target at close range. Extensive dry-fire and live-fire training will enable you to go from a ready position to a shooting position with the sights seemingly pre-aligned on the target. This can be achieved most readily if your shooting position is consistent and you use proper grip alignment, correct trigger finger placement, and your natural point of aim (NPA).

Remember, too, that distance equals time. In general, the farther away a threat is, the more time you will have to acquire proper sight alignment before shooting. At the same time, as the distance to your target increases, the more critical proper sight alignment becomes in achieving a hit.

# POINT SHOOTING

Sometimes an attack occurs so close and so fast that any reference to sight alignment becomes unnecessary or impossible. *Point shooting* is the technique used in such circumstances.

Point shooting involves simply raising or extending the handgun from a ready position to your normal two-handed firing stance, with the muzzle pointed toward the center of mass of the target, and firing as soon as your arms are in the shooting position. There is no attempt whatsoever to visually align the front and rear sights, or the sights with the target.

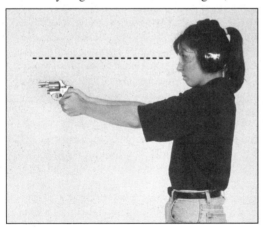

You are focused on the target instead of the sights; specifically, you are focused on the precise area—the center of exposed mass—you want the bullet to strike. Although you are not actively using the sights, the handgun will be at eye level and you likely will be aware of at least the rear sight in your peripheral vision. Also, you will perceive (in your peripheral vision) the general outline of the firearm,

*Fig. 45. The two-handed point shooting position, viewed from the side. Note that the shooter's line of sight is above the sights of the handgun.*

The Basics of Personal Protection in the Home

and use that outline as a visual reference to roughly align the gun with the target.

The use of a thumb-forward two-handed grip (taught in the NRA Basic Pistol Course) aids in point shooting by allowing you to "point" with the support hand thumb, which is held parallel to the barrel.

# MULTIPLE SHOTS

As has been mentioned elsewhere in this book, you should not expect to stop a vicious attacking criminal with a single shot. Typically, several shots with a handgun are required to end a violent assault. Thus, you must learn techniques for delivering multiple shots accurately and rapidly.

The majority of defensive shooting instructors recommend that the armed citizen shoot until the assailant no longer presents a deadly threat. In training drills, two rapid initial hits on the target are often required, not because there is any special magic about the number two, but because two-shot drills allow the simulation of multiple shot firing sequences without unduly wasting ammunition.

After firing, briefly assess the target to determine if a threat still exists and additional shots are required. This focus on firing multiple shots gives rise to specific shooting techniques designed to maximize the hit probability of rounds fired in quick succession.

Effective multiple-shot shooting involves techniques that may be modified depending upon the speed of shooting required by the situation. When great accuracy is required—such as when a target is located at longer ranges (generally 10-15 yards or more) or when only a small amount of target mass is exposed—good sight alignment is required, and shots are fired in succession as quickly as you can recover the proper sight alignment. The speed with which you can fire such shots depends upon your ability to recover from recoil, re-establish proper sight alignment, breath control, hold control and NPA, and execute the shot using proper trigger control and follow-through. Remember, all the shooting fundamentals still apply; they are simply compressed to allow faster shooting.

*Fig. 46. Your practice should regularly include multiple-shot drills that emphasize both speed and accuracy.*

To engage targets at closer range (such as 3-7 yards), multiple shots may be fired more quickly. To execute such shots, a flash sight picture is used instead of refined sight alignment and the sequence of trigger pull, firing and follow-through for each shot is accelerated. The speed with which such accelerated shots can be fired varies with individual skill and experience; most people execute these shots more quickly than the aimed shots required at longer ranges. However, the shot dispersion of accelerated shots is generally greater than with aimed shots, making the multiple-shot technique more difficult, for most shooters, when the target is distant or only slightly exposed.

When a violent attack occurs quickly, at extremely close range, the multiple-shot technique can be further accelerated to allow successive hits on the target in the least possible time.

At extremely close range (3 yards and less), shots can be fired once you have established a flash sight picture, or, in situations essentially at arm's length, can be fired as a variation of point shooting. In both cases, the second and successive shots are fired in rapid succession without any conscious attempt to align the sights. "Aiming" of successive shots is done essentially by feel, using muscle memory; these shots are fired as soon as you sense that the gun has returned from the recoil of the preceding shot and is again pointed at the target. With most defensive handguns having moderate recoil, successive shots can be fired essentially as quickly as you can pull the trigger.

Note that the various shooting fundamentals are either modified or substantially compressed as the speed with which multiple shots are fired increases. However, good trigger control is still essential. Even though the trigger pull is accelerated to the point of being almost a slap, there will still be little or no gun movement or misalignment of the sights if the trigger finger is properly located on the trigger.

With considerable practice, these highly accelerated shots can be fired extremely quickly and with surprising accuracy. Skilled practical pistol shooters can trigger two shots with an interval of .20 second or less, and place them only a couple of inches apart on a target 5 to 7 yards away. Such ability is the result of the development of a high level of coordination and the mastery of both the shooting fundamentals and the elements of a proper shooting position, allowing successive shots to be fired immediately as the gun returns to its original firing position. Frequent, focused practice—both live- and dry-fire—is the only way to achieve this level of skill.

This technique of firing quick, accurate multiple shots should be reserved for encounters occurring at very close range—from arm's length to not more than three or four yards. Using the technique at longer ranges creates the risk of wild shots that could endanger an innocent bystander.

When practicing, experiment with different cadences for each multiple-shot technique and distance, and note which produces the closest groups.

# MULTIPLE ASSAILANTS

Crime statistics indicate the growing prevalence of attacks involving more than one assailant. Although the same basic defensive shooting skills are used whether you are facing one violent criminal or several, successfully defeating multiple adversaries involves a slightly different kind of threat assessment.

When confronted with multiple assailants, the primary rule is to engage

*Fig. 47. In the case of multiple assailants, you may have to assess the relative threat posed by each assailant, and respond accordingly. Here, the closer of the two attackers is wielding a knife, while the other attacker has a handgun in his waistband. In this case the attacker closest to you may represent the greater threat, even though he is armed with a seemingly less effective weapon than his partner.*

the targets in the order of the greatest threat. For example, if you encounter two intruders in your home, one armed with a gun and one with a piece of pipe, you would normally engage the gun-wielding criminal first. Factors involved in threat assessment include:

- the distance of each attacker;
- the type of weapon possessed by each attacker; and
- the mobility of each attacker.

The attacker armed with a gun may not always represent the greatest threat, however. An intruder with an upraised baseball bat, running at you aggressively from only a few yards away, may be more of an immediate threat than his accomplice, 10 yards away and with his gun stuck in his waistband.

In assessing any threat, whether single or multiple assailants, train yourself to always look at the hands of your attackers; that is where the threat will come from. Be suspicious of hands kept where you cannot see them, such as in pockets, alongside the thigh or behind the back. For example, an attacker armed with a knife may hide his weapon by hanging the hand down naturally, just out of sight behind the thigh. In this fashion it does not appear that he is hiding anything, but the knife can be brought up in a deadly thrust before you can react to it. Always assume that hands that are out of sight contain a weapon.

When visualizing a multiple-adversary attack, or when practicing at the range using multiple targets, keep both the target distance and your gun's magazine capacity in mind. Both affect how you decide to engage the targets. If all targets are close, it may be preferable to engage each target with one round and then assess the remaining threats, rather than put two shots on each threat. If you try to engage each of three targets with two shots, for example, you may allow the last threat to rush and kill or injure you, or to use his weapon against you, while you are firing at the first two assailants. Also, if your firearm has a very limited capacity, you may run out of ammunition before engaging all targets if you choose to fire two shots at each threat.

*Fig. 48. A casual pose can conceal a deadly threat. At left, the individual lounges against a wall, his hands seemingly empty. However, when his right hand is rotated forward (right), a large folding knife is shown to be concealed in his palm.*

The Basics of Personal Protection in the Home

# TUNNEL VISION

During a life-threatening confrontation, you likely will be affected by *tunnel vision*—the tendency to concentrate on the target to the exclusion of everything else around you. This phenomenon is made worse by high stress levels. Tunnel vision can persist for several moments even after the encounter has been resolved, whether that resolution involves the assailant fleeing, surrendering, or being shot by you. In all of these circumstances, you will tend to keep focused on the area from which the threat came— even if that means staring out the door a home intruder just exited through. While you are experiencing tunnel vision, you are vulnerable to attack by additional, unseen assailants.

To maintain maximum alertness and readiness, you must train to first lower the gun and then scan the area to the left and right of the target area once you determine that a threat is no longer present. Then perform a 360-degree visual scan of the area to search for additional threats.

During the process of scanning the area, the gun is dropped to the ready position and pointed in the direction of the original threat, (in case they become a threat again) and the head and eyes move independently of the gun. If a new threat is identified, the gun is directed to the new threat.

This procedure for assessing the area for additional threats is performed whether you have just finished firing a string of shots that has downed an assailant, or your attacker has fled through a window. However, in situations in which your attacker has surrendered and has

*Fig. 49. To maintain maximum alertness after an attack is stopped, first lower the gun and then scan to the right and left of the target area once you determine that a threat is no longer present. The target is kept in view in the peripheral vision.*

assumed the proper submission position on the floor (see Chapter 15: Confronting an Intruder or Attacker), you should minimize the period of time your eyes are off him. Removing your eyes from the surrendered assailant to scan the area behind you may give him the opportunity to resume the attack on you. When you are covering a surrendered attacker, back up against a wall to eliminate the possibility of being attacked directly from the rear by an unseen assailant, and then scan as far left and right as possible without losing sight of the surrendered criminal in your peripheral vision. In this way, you will be aware of any movement the attacker makes. If it is not possible to back up to a wall, you must scan the area behind you. This scan should be performed as quickly as possible to minimize the time the surrendered assailant is out of your view.

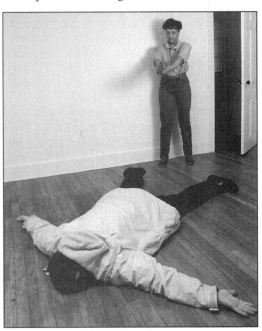

Fig. 50. When you are covering a surrendered or downed attacker, back up against the wall and be sure to keep your assailant in view at all times.

# CHAPTER 10

# UTILIZING COVER AND CONCEALMENT

Shooting skill is only one of the factors that determine whether you prevail in a violent encounter. Of equal importance are the strategies you use to minimize the threat posed by your assailant and maximize the effectiveness of the response you make.

When you anticipate being confronted by an armed attacker, the most immediate tactical response you should make is to seek *cover* or

*Fig. 51. An intruder's-eye view of a basement room, showing a home defender (inset, arrow) making good use of concealment.*

*concealment.* In motion pictures and on television, people often seek cover or concealment only after they are shot at. In the real world, however, you should seek cover or concealment whenever there is a likelihood of

encountering an aggressor. For example, if you hear a suspicious rustling in the bushes as you go up the walk to your front door late at night, you should immediately retreat to a position of cover. Don't just stand there in the open and give a potential attacker the advantage of a clear shot at you. A protected position allows you to more safely assess the situation and decide upon your course of action.

The concepts of cover and concealment are sometimes used interchangeably, but actually are very different. *Cover* is anything that will protect all or part of your body from incoming fire. *Concealment*, on the other hand, is anything that will hide all or part of your body from observation. An object that provides concealment will not protect your body from incoming fire. By definition, objects that provide concealment do not necessarily provide cover. Objects affording cover, however, usually provide some level of concealment.

*Fig. 52. This home defender is using the cover afforded by a full, heavy steel file cabinet. The file cabinet both hides the homeowner and affords protection from shots fired by an assailant.*

The importance of cover lies in its ability to prevent injury during a violent confrontation. Avoiding injury during an attack is critical, not merely because of the likelihood of pain, permanent damage, or even death that results from a wound from a weapon, but also because studies have shown that injury decreases the ability of the intended victim to fight back and survive the attack. Anything you can do to minimize your risk of injury during an encounter with an attacker will increase the chance that you and your loved ones will prevail.

Cover provides protection not only from an assailant armed with a gun, but also from one using other weapons or even bare hands. At close range, a knife or baseball bat can be as deadly as a firearm. By putting a hard object between you and your assailant, you may be able to avoid injury while gaining time to escape or, as a last resort, to employ your firearm.

Concealment can help prevent an assailant from locating you or directing accurate fire at you. Proper utilization of concealment may also allow you to gain the advantage of surprise over an attacker, or allow you to avoid or escape an attacker completely. Even when your assailant knows you are somewhere in the vicinity—in the same room, for example—your use of concealment gives you a practical advantage.

It is almost always preferable to seek cover rather than concealment. Items providing cover usually afford some level of concealment as well, so the choice between cover and concealment is usually not an "either-or" proposition. In defensive shooting situations, however, there are few absolute rules, and there may be occasions when it is preferable to choose a position offering concealment rather than one offering cover. For example, if a concealment position affords a better escape route, less exposure to a second attacker, or a better firing position than a position behind cover, you should choose the concealment position.

# OBJECTS PROVIDING COVER AND CONCEALMENT

Every home contains objects that can provide either cover or concealment, or both. Items providing concealment don't necessarily need to be large enough to hide your entire body. In a pinch, even relatively small things—such as a wastebasket, folding chair, coffee table or cardboard box—can disguise your outline, preventing an attacker from

immediately detecting you and giving you the advantage of surprise, however briefly. This is particularly true under low-light conditions. In general, larger objects, such as sofas, file cabinets or refrigerators are preferred for concealment purposes.

Whether a given object can provide cover— protection from incoming fire—depends upon a number of factors. The cartridge for which your attacker's firearm is

*Fig. 53. A long, heavy object, such as this dresser or a full bookcase, can provide cover–but only if the defender positions him- or herself to use its length to stop a bullet.*

chambered is one such factor; an object that defeats a bullet from a .22 rimfire might be easily penetrated by a bullet from a .357 Magnum. Also, the more material that must be penetrated by the bullet, the better cover is afforded. An empty file cabinet with walls of thin-gauge steel provides little or no protection from even low-powered cartridges; filled tightly with files, however, it may completely defeat many handgun rounds. Angle of entry is also critical. A bookcase full of books, shot front to back, provides little protection. Shot from side to side (lengthwise), however, with the bullet traversing several feet of books, the bookcase may provide more cover, but less concealment.

Objects that most people might intuitively think of as providing cover may, in fact, provide little protection. For example, a standard interior sheetrock or plaster wall will not reliably stop even a .22 rimfire bullet; neither will most sofas, chairs, tables, cabinets and the like. Even a thick hardwood door may be penetrated by a jacketed bullet from a moderate-power cartridge, such as a .38 Spl. or 9mm Parabellum. A standard mattress provides little cover, unless shot in a lengthwise direction. A waterbed mattress may provide cover, but only as long as it contains enough water to stop a bullet.

Fig. 54. A typical room in a home, showing several objects capable of providing concealment, including two large chairs, a credenza and a sofa. None of these items, however, would provide cover.

Though most homes contain many things capable of providing concealment or partial cover, there are relatively few household objects capable of providing complete cover. Metal objects such as gun safes or free-standing iron or steel wood stoves can provide such protection, as can some older, heavier appliances (particularly if you position yourself behind a motor or compressor). Interior brick, stone or concrete-block walls can also provide complete cover. However, even such walls, as well as many other types of cover, can be defeated by repeated bullet strikes to the same spot.

Even if they are unable to provide complete protection from incoming fire, many objects in the home can nonetheless provide limited cover—that is, they are capable of deflecting or slowing a bullet and decreasing its injury-causing potential. While it is always preferable to seek cover behind items affording complete protection, this may not always be possible. Limited cover is better than no cover at all.

Even when no adequate cover is available, you should still endeavor to conceal yourself behind any available object. The less of you an attacker sees, the less of you there is to aim at—and the harder you are to hit. Furthermore, in the heat of a violent confrontation, your assailant may not have the presence of mind to realize that you are still vulnerable behind a wooden door or sheetrock wall, and instead may try to hit only that part of your body that is exposed.

As part of your personal protection plan, perform a survey of your home to determine which objects may provide cover or concealment. Assess each item for the level of protection it may afford and its placement in relation to possible lines of attack and retreat. It may be desirable to rearrange certain items to maximize their usefulness in providing cover or concealment, particularly in the safe room in your home (see Chapter 13: Making You and Your Home Safer).

# PLANNING LOCATIONS
# FOR COVER AND CONCEALMENT

*Fig. 55. To scan around a corner or doorway for possible danger, bob your head to the side rapidly to take a "quick peek" of the area. By minimizing your exposure and varying where your head will appear, you prevent yourself from becoming an easy target.*

If possible, place items affording cover or concealment in locations offering a clear lane of fire at the probable entry point of an attacker, as well as an escape route allowing you to retreat to a position of safety. Avoid seeking cover in locations in which you would be vulnerable from attack by a second assailant.

Make use of natural shadows and less-illuminated areas when selecting locations for your cover and concealment. Select spots having a background that tends to break up your outline; avoid rear illumination that can clearly silhouette you.

Don't forget safety when choosing spots for cover or concealment. A full fuel oil tank in the basement, for example, might well stop a handgun bullet, but oil that spills from a perforated tank creates a serious fire hazard.

# TECHNIQUES FOR USING COVER AND CONCEALMENT

Whether waiting for an intruder's approach in the dark or returning fire, it is critically important to minimize your exposure. The less of you that is visible, the greater your chance of escaping detection and gaining the element of surprise. Even in the event that shots are fired, minimizing your exposure will make you a more difficult target to aim at, and will decrease your chance of being hit.

At times you may not be able to immediately see around a corner of a hallway, edge of a door, etc. Rather than slowly peering around the obstruction (which would allow an attacker time to detect and take aim at you), use a quick peek to scan the area. Rapidly bob your head to the side just enough to get a "snapshot" of the area and just as quickly tuck it back behind cover. Your total exposure should be considerably less than a second—too little time for an armed adversary to see you and react with an accurate shot. Also, vary the location you peek from. If you take several quick peeks from the same location, an assailant may pre-aim at that spot and be ready to fire at your next appearance.

*Fig. 56 The "leaning out" technique allows you to fire effectively while minimizing exposure.*

On those occasions when it is essential to avoid being spotted behind cover or concealment, it is important to keep still. The eye is very sensitive to motion; a slight bob of the head or movement of the gun may draw an attacker's attention and give away your location.

When you must fire from cover, there are several important techniques you should utilize. To minimize exposure while firing from behind cover in a standing two-handed position, use the *leaning out* technique. First, assume the proper two-handed stance behind cover. Then, simply tilt or lean your upper body to the right or left (as necessary) just enough to acquire the target. Note that when leaning out to the weak-hand side, you should not grip the firearm in your weak hand. The strong-hand grip is maintained, and you simply lean out as needed to acquire the target.

The Basics of Personal Protection in the Home

The gun may be canted slightly, and your body will be slightly more exposed than when shooting from the strong side. When practicing the "leaning out" technique, be conscious of the amount of body mass that is exposed from each side, and adjust your position so as to keep as much of your body as possible behind cover.

When shooting multiple shots from cover, avoid emerging from the same point every time you fire. Typically, as with the quick peek technique used to observe an area from behind cover, you should emerge only long enough to acquire the target and fire accurately (in most cases with a single assailant, a rapid pair of shots) and then duck back behind cover. When you re-emerge for subsequent shots, vary the point from which you fire. This may necessitate using different shooting positions (kneeling, standing, etc.) from behind cover.

It is also critical to ensure that the gun's muzzle is clear of the cover. Whether shooting over an object, such

*Fig. 57. The muzzle should always be kept well clear of any object providing cover or concealment.*

as a countertop or desk, or around the side of a wall or piece of furniture, it is easy to lose track of the location of the gun's muzzle. Under the stress of a defensive encounter, both inexperienced and experienced shooters may assume that because the sights are clear of cover, the muzzle must also be clear. This is particularly true when the shooter cants the gun to minimize exposure from behind cover. Firing into cover has several potentially harmful effects. First and foremost, shooting a bullet into certain types of cover at extremely close range—a matter of inches—may result in serious injury to the shooter, either from bullet ricochet or backspatter or from flying fragments from the cover itself. Firing into your own cover can also reduce its effectiveness in protecting you. Furthermore, a bullet that passes through or is deflected by cover is extremely unlikely to find its target — your assailant.

Moreover, it is important to avoid resting or bracing the handgun on or against cover. Contact with cover can impede the rotation of the cylinder of a revolver or the operation of the slide of a semi-automatic; both conditions can cause gun failures. Even when contact with cover does not cause gun malfunctions, that contact often degrades accuracy by causing shots to be thrown wide. Take care to prevent the firearm from banging against cover during recoil. This is particularly important when firing through a narrow horizontal port, such as under the corner of a bed. If the muzzle protrudes through the port, recoil can smash the front sight against the cover object, possibly damaging the

*Fig. 58. Above, a defensive shooter should not allow the muzzle of his or her handgun to protrude beyond the object providing cover or concealment. Left, when firing a semi-automatic pistol from the left side of a barricade, the pistol should be canted slightly to the left. This changes the trajectory of the ejected cases and reduces the likelihood of a case bouncing off the barricade and back into the ejection port, jamming the gun.*

sight or preventing normal slide travel, or both.

You can avoid the problems caused by gun contact with cover by staying back from the cover at least far enough to prevent the gun's muzzle from protruding beyond it. Maintaining this distance will also often provide you with better mobility and greater concealment and protection.

Since most semi-automatic pistols eject to the right, special care must be taken when firing a semi-automatic pistol from the left side of cover. With the pistol held vertically close to cover, an ejected case can bounce off the object providing cover and into the ejection port, jamming the pistol. To prevent this, a semi-automatic pistol fired from the left side of a barricade or other cover should be canted to move the ejection port away from the cover and to produce an ejection trajectory that will minimize the chance for case bounce-back.

Keep in mind that the various positions used for shooting from cover share the same basic characteristics as other shooting positions:

- consistency;
- balance;
- support;
- Natural Point of Aim (NPA); and
- comfort.

# MOVEMENT TO COVER
# AND CONCEALMENT

In any defensive encounter, try to keep as much distance as possible between you and your assailant. When your assailant is unarmed or armed only with a club, knife, tire iron or the like, increasing your distance from him or her may remove you from immediate harm and give you the opportunity to escape the encounter or, if that is impossible, to take appropriate measures to stop the attack. An unarmed attacker who is allowed to approach too closely may succeed in blocking your firearm or taking it from you. Even when your attacker has a firearm, it still makes sense to move away as far and as quickly as possible, for your chance of being hit by an assailant's bullet diminishes with increasing distance.

During an encounter with an aggressor, try to move not only *away* from that person, but also *toward* a source of cover. Again, remember that you should not wait until you are shot at or otherwise attacked to seek cover. Also, always seek cover after you have fired shots, even if your shots seem to have stopped the attack. Just because an assailant has gone down and appears incapacitated does not mean he or she is no longer dangerous. Your attacker may be stunned or shamming, or may suddenly "come around" with a burst of violent energy.

You should practice moving backward and laterally toward cover. There are specific techniques for both types of movement, which allow you to maintain your:

- *view of your assailant* or of an area (a doorway, window, etc.) where that assailant may appear;
- *firearm in a ready position* or shooting position for the quickest possible shot if necessary; and
- *balance* while moving, preventing stumbling on obstacles or making unnecessary sound.

Movement—either backward or lateral—is a good idea after firing shots, even if the distance moved is only a few feet. As noted previously, many violent attacks occur in low light, and an assailant may be able to pinpoint your position primarily through your muzzle flashes. Changing position will make it more difficult for an assailant to locate you.

**Moving Backward.** The proper technique for moving backward can be thought of as resembling the exaggerated walk performed by Groucho Marx in the various Marx Brothers motion pictures. The knees are bent and the hips are lowered, making your center of gravity lower and increasing stability during movement. Your eyes are kept focused on the assailant or on the area from which danger may come.

Movement is commenced by extending your lead foot rearward with

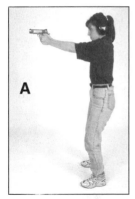
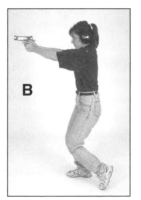

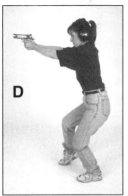
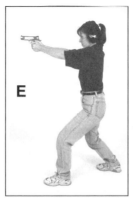

Fig. 59. Moving backward. (A) From a shooting position, (B) lift the lead foot and slide it rearward with the toe down and heel raised to allow the foot to detect obstacles while the eyes remain on the threat. (C) When the foot is planted flat on the ground the body's weight can be transferred to that foot. (D & E) Repeat the process until you can reach cover and resume a shooting position.

the toe down and the heel high to feel for obstacles. This is necessary because you may be required to move in darkness or low light, and in any event must not look away from the assailant or danger zone to check for obstructions or debris. When the toe contacts the floor, the rest of the sole of the foot rolls down until the heel touches the floor. Your weight should not shift to the rear foot until that foot is fully flat on the ground. In this way, if the foot encounters an obstacle or an uneven surface, you can move it to a different location that is clear of debris without causing a loss of balance. After the lead foot has been placed firmly on the ground, the same procedure is repeated with the other foot.

Avoid shooting while moving. The proper procedure is to shoot, move, shoot, then move again. Shooting while on the move—an advanced skill—almost always results in poor marksmanship, wasted shots and potential danger to innocent bystanders.

**Moving Laterally.** When cover is located off to one side, rather than to the rear, or when you find yourself backed up against a wall, only lateral

The Basics of Personal Protection in the Home

Fig. 60. Moving laterally. (A) From a shooting position, bend the knees and drop the hips. (B) Extend the lead foot to the side with the outside edge up to detect obstacles. (C) When the foot is at shoulder width, plant it flat on the ground and transfer the body's weight to both feet. (D) Slide the trailing foot inward (E) next to the lead foot. Repeat until you can reach cover and resume a firing position.

movement may be possible. To move laterally, first bend your knees and drop your hips (though not as much as when moving rearward). Then extend the lead foot to the side with the outside edge held high in order to feel for obstacles. The inside edge of the lead foot plants in position first, and the foot rolls to the outside edge as the weight is shifted to the foot. Do not shift your weight to the lead foot until that foot is fully flat on the ground. In this way, if your foot encounters an obstacle or an uneven surface, you can move it to a different location that is clear of debris without causing a loss of balance.

Note that the feet do not cross during this lateral movement. Once the lead foot is planted, the trailing foot is brought inward only until it can be planted alongside the extended lead foot. The lead foot extends again, repeating the process. The trailing foot never crosses or passes the lead foot. As with backward movement, avoid shooting while moving. The proper procedure is to shoot, move, shoot, then move again.

# CHAPTER 11

# GUN HANDLING

Most defensive-oriented gun owners recognize the importance of mastering the fundamentals of shooting and the various shooting positions. Often neglected, however, are those skills collectively known as *gun handling skills*. These include reloading techniques and procedures for quickly clearing stoppages and resolving other gun malfunctions.

## RELOADING

As used in the NRA Basic Personal Protection in the Home Course, *reloading* means refilling an empty gun with cartridges as quickly as possible. There are specific methods for reloading both revolvers and semi-automatic pistols, and for both right- and left-handed shooters.

Whenever possible, reload while you are behind cover. Reloading while out in the open exposes you to your attacker when you cannot fire back. Furthermore, during reloading you must momentarily take your eyes off the target or target area. It is generally safer to do this behind cover.

In some situations you may use reloading techniques to reload a gun that is only partially empty. For example, in a situation in which you fire five rounds from a six-shot revolver and then retreat to cover, use the temporary breathing space that cover affords to reload your revolver and bring it back to full capacity. Do not be concerned with the single live round you dump out on the floor with the five empty cases.

### Reloading the Revolver With Speedloaders

The fastest way to reload a revolver is through the use of a *speedloader*, a mechanical device that holds a number of cartridges in a pattern that aligns them with the chambers of the revolver. The speed loader (pictured at right) allows the cartridges to be inserted simultaneously into the cylinder chambers, at which point they are released and the revolver is completely reloaded.

Revolver shooters not having speedloaders must reload using loose rounds from a pocket. Right-handed shooters should put their loose rounds in a right-side pocket, while left-handed shooters should put them in a left-side

*Fig. 61. Speedloaders.*

pocket. Any pocket that contains extra ammunition, whether in the form of loose rounds or speed loaders, should not have anything else in it. This prevents fumbling for ammunition or inadvertently attempting to load the revolver with coins, chewing gum, lip balm, lipstick or anything else that may be in the pocket.

# Reloading the Revolver (Right-Handed Technique)

Beginning with the revolver held in a two-hand firing grip in the right hand, pointed in a safe direction and the finger off the trigger (A), bend the elbows to bring the revolver back close to the body at about chest height

and slightly to the right of the centerline of the torso (B). Keep your eyes on the target area throughout the procedure except when you are actually inserting cartridges into the chambers.

As the gun is being brought back (just as the elbow of the firing arm begins to bend), cup the left hand underneath the trigger guard area of the frame of the revolver. Grasp the cylinder between the two middle fingers and the thumb of the left hand (C). Viewed from the rear, the thumb contacts the cylinder at the 9 o'clock position, while the two middle fingers make contact at the 3

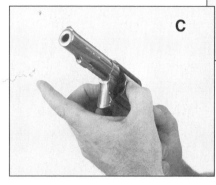

o'clock position. The bottom of the trigger guard is over the palm of the left hand. Care must be taken, particularly with short-barreled revolvers, to keep the left index finger clear of the muzzle.

With the cylinder thus firmly

The Basics of Personal Protection in the Home

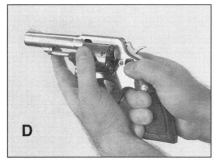

**D**

grasped by the left hand, the right thumb engages the cylinder release (D). Twist the right wrist to rotate the frame 90 degrees clockwise. The two middle fingers of the left hand pass through the frame; the grip is maintained on the cylinder by the thumb and two middle fingers of the left hand. It is important to rotate the frame away from the cylinder rather than simply push the cylinder out of the frame. The cylinder is held stationary by the left hand while the right hand rotates the frame away from the cylinder.

As the revolver frame is rotated away from the cylinder, roll your left wrist slightly toward you to direct the muzzle almost straight upward. Be sure to keep the muzzle angled away from you. Let go of the revolver with the right hand and maintain your hold of the cylinder with the fingers and thumb of the left hand still in the 3 and 9 o'clock positions (E). The left elbow should now be close to or touching the abdomen and the revolver should still be positioned to the right of the centerline of the body, just below the armpit.

**E**

With the inside of the palm of the right hand, strike the ejector rod with

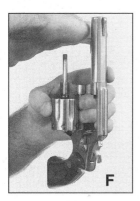

**F**

**G**

a straight, sharp downward blow (F, G). The rod should contact the palm at a point midway along an imaginary line between the base of the pinky finger and the center of the wrist joint.

**CAUTION:** Strike the ejector hard enough to throw the empty cases well clear of the cylinder with the first blow, but not so hard as to injure your hand or bend the ejector rod. In guns with dirty or scored cylinders, or when higher-pressure loads are used, the first sharp blow to the ejector rod may push the cases only part way out of their chambers in the cylinder. A second or third sharp blow may be required for full, forceful ejection.

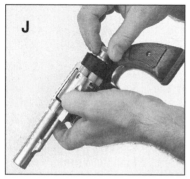

Allow the empty cases to fall free of the cylinder to the ground. Do not attempt to retrieve the cases (or any live rounds you may also eject from the cylinder).

As your right hand reaches for a speedloader, or loose cartridges in your pocket, bring the revolver in front of you at about chest height, rotating the muzzle downward and away from you (H). Retrieve a

speedloader or one or two loose cartridges from your pocket with your right hand and bring that hand to the revolver just above the cylinder.

If you are using a speedloader, look down briefly as you align the cartridges with the cylinder's chambers (I). A momentary glance to ensure that the cylinder

is indeed empty, and that the nose of each bullet has entered the chamber properly (J) is sufficient. Then release the cartridges into the chambers and drop the speedloader to the ground.

If you are loading loose cartridges, grasp them at the rim using your thumb and forefinger. Seat them with the

The Basics of Personal Protection in the Home

thumb as they enter the chamber. With practice, you can load two cartridges at a time by grasping them at their rims using the thumb and first two fingers and inserting them simultaneously into adjacent chambers. When loading loose cartridges it is more efficient to remove only one or two at a time from the pocket, load them and then go back to the pocket for one or two more, rather than grabbing five or six cartridges at one time.

When reloading with either a speed loader or loose cartridges, dirty cylinder walls or a cartridge that is slightly oversize or out of round may cause you to feel some resistance while chambering one or more cartridges. It is important to ensure that all cartridges are fully seated in the cylinder. Cartridges that protrude from their chambers can keep the cylinder from closing or rotating.

Once the cartridges are seated in their chambers in the cylinder, grasp the grip portion of the frame in a firing grip with the right hand. Remember to keep the trigger finger indexed along the side of the frame, out of the trigger guard. As you start to raise the revolver (still keeping the muzzle in a downward direction to keep

the cartridges from falling out of their chambers), rotate the frame counter-clockwise with the right wrist while simultaneously pushing the cylinder home with the left thumb (K). You will hear a click as the cylinder latch catches. As the cylinder clicks shut, rotate the cylinder with the thumb and middle fingers until it locks into place with a cartridge directly under the firing pin (L). If you fail to properly index the cylinder with a chamber under the firing pin, the gun may not fire when the trigger is pulled.

Once the cylinder is securely shut and indexed to put a cartridge under the firing pin, raise the muzzle into alignment with the target. The left hand slides back over the right into its supporting grip position and the firing position is once again assumed, and you assess the target area (M).

# Reloading the Revolver
# (Left-Handed Technique)

Beginning with the revolver held in a two-hand firing grip in the left hand, pointed in a safe direction and the finger off the trigger (A), bend the elbows to bring the revolver back close to the body at about chest height and to the left of the centerline of the torso (B). Keep your eyes on the target area except when you are inserting cartridges into the chambers.

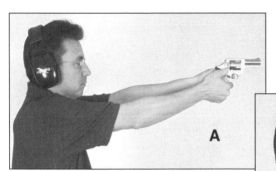

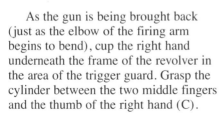

As the gun is being brought back (just as the elbow of the firing arm begins to bend), cup the right hand underneath the frame of the revolver in the area of the trigger guard. Grasp the cylinder between the two middle fingers and the thumb of the right hand (C).

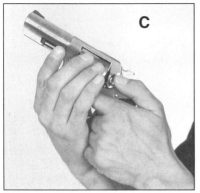

Viewed from the rear, the thumb contacts the cylinder at the 3 o'clock position, while the two middle fingers make contact at the 9 o'clock position. The bottom of the trigger guard is over the bottom of the right hand. Care must be taken, particularly with short-barreled revolvers, to keep the right index finger clear of the muzzle.

While maintaining grip pressure with the three fingers of the left

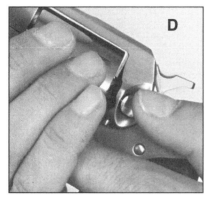

hand, bring the left thumb around to the left side of the frame and engage the cylinder release (D). Twist the left wrist to rotate the frame 90 degrees clockwise. The thumb of the right hand passes through the frame; the grip is maintained on the cylinder by the thumb and two middle fingers of the right hand. It is important to rotate the frame away from the cylinder rather than simply push

the cylinder out of the frame. The cylinder is held stationary by the right hand while the left hand rotates the frame away from the cylinder (E).

As the revolver frame is rotated away from the cylinder, roll your right wrist slightly toward you to direct the muzzle almost straight upward. Be sure to keep the muzzle angled away from you. Let go of the revolver with the left hand and

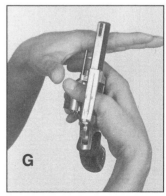

maintain your hold of the cylinder with the fingers and thumb of the right hand still in the 3 and 9 o'clock positions. The right elbow should now be close to or touching the abdomen and the revolver should still be positioned to the left of the centerline of the body.

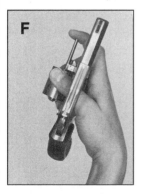

There are two methods for actuating the ejector rod. Push the ejector rod firmly with the index finger of the right hand (F), or strike it with a straight, sharp blow with the inside of the palm of the left hand (G). The rod should contact the left palm at a point directly below the base of the index finger. The latter method is more likely to eject cases from the cylinder.

**CAUTION:** Strike the ejector hard enough to throw the empty cases well clear of the cylinder with the first blow, but not so hard as to injure your hand or bend the ejector rod. In guns with dirty or scored cylinders, or when higher-pressure loads are used, the first sharp blow to the ejector rod may push the cases only part way out of their chambers in the cylinder. A second or third sharp blow may be required for full ejection.

Allow the empty cases to fall free of the cylinder and hit the ground. Do not attempt to retrieve the cases (or any live rounds you may also eject from the cylinder).

As your left hand reaches for a speedloader or loose cartridges in your pocket, bring the revolver in front of you at about chest height, simultaneously rotating the muzzle downward and away from you (H). Retrieve a speed loader or one or two loose cartridges from your pocket with your left hand and bring that hand to the revolver just above the cylinder.

If you are using a speed loader, look down briefly as you align the cartridges with the cylinder's chambers (I). A momentary glance to ensure that the nose of each bullet has entered the chamber (J) is sufficient. Then release the cartridges into the chambers (K)

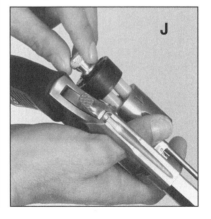

The Basics of Personal Protection in the Home

and drop the speed loader to the ground.

If you are loading loose cartridges, grasp them at the rim using your thumb and forefinger. Seat them with the thumb as they enter the chamber. With practice, you can load two cartridges at a time by grasping them at their rims using the thumb and first two fingers and inserting them simultaneously into adjacent chambers. When loading loose cartridges it is more efficient to remove only one or two at a time from the pocket, load them and then go back to the pocket for one or two more, rather than grabbing many cartridges at one time (L).

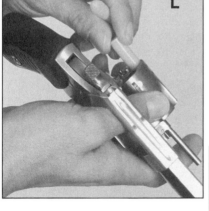

When reloading with either a speed loader or loose cartridges, dirty cylinder walls or a cartridge that is slightly oversize or out of round may cause you to feel some resistance while chambering one or more cartridges. It is important to ensure that all cartridges are fully seated in their chambers in the cylinder. Cartridges that protrude from their chambers can keep the cylinder from closing or rotating.

Once the cartridges are seated in their chambers in the cylinder, grasp the grip portion of the frame in a firing grip with the left hand. Remember to keep the trigger finger indexed along the side of the frame, out of the trigger guard. As you start to raise the revolver (still keeping the muzzle in a downward direction to

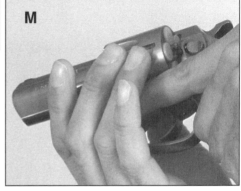

keep the cartridges from falling out of their chambers), rotate the frame counter-clockwise with the left wrist while simultaneously pushing the cylinder home with the right fingers (M). You will hear a click as the cylinder latch

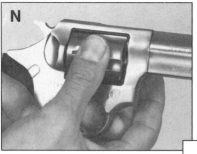

catches. As the cylinder clicks shut, rotate the cylinder with the thumb and middle fingers until it locks into place with a cartridge directly under the firing pin (N). If you fail to properly index the cylinder with a chamber under the firing pin, the gun may not fire when the trigger is pulled.

Once the cylinder is securely shut and indexed to put a cartridge under the firing pin, raise the muzzle into alignment with the target. The right hand slides back over the left into its supporting grip position and the firing position is once again assumed, and you assess the target area (O).

# Reloading the Semi-Automatic Pistol (Right-Handed Technique)

Beginning with the pistol held in a firing grip, trigger finger indexed alongside the frame, and the muzzle pointed in a safe direction (A), bend the elbows to bring the pistol close to the body (B). The elbow of the shooting arm should be close to or in contact with the torso. The muzzle should point upward and away from you (or, if upward is not a safe direction, toward the target).

As you bring the pistol in close to your body, place the tip of the thumb of the right hand on the magazine release button (assuming the button is

The Basics of Personal Protection in the Home

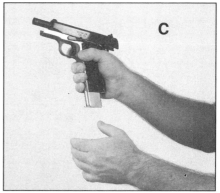

located in the usual position on the left side of the frame just to the rear of the trigger guard). It may be necessary to shift the right hand grip to allow the thumb to reach the release button. Press the magazine release button straight into the frame and hold it in while the magazine drops free of the frame (C). You should be able to glimpse the falling magazine in your peripheral vision. Do not attempt to retrieve the ejected magazine.

If the magazine does not fall free of the frame of its own weight, swiftly strip it from the pistol with the left hand and drop it on the ground.

At the same time, the left (support) hand reaches for a loaded

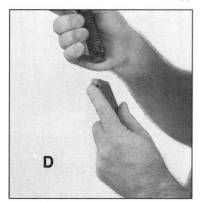

magazine. Grasp the magazine between the thumb and middle finger, with the floorplate (base) of the magazine in the palm of the hand and the index finger running up the front of the magazine body, resting on or just below the tip of the bullet of the top cartridge (D).

As the firing hand continues to bring the pistol in toward the torso, rotate the right hand wrist 90 degrees so that the left side of the frame faces you and the pistol is just below eye level (E). At the same time, the left hand brings the magazine close to the magazine well of the pistol.

Keep visual focus on the target area during these steps.

Glance down briefly at the magazine well, both to ensure that it is clear of an empty magazine and to locate it visually to facilitate magazine insertion (F). Using the left-hand index finger on the magazine to "point" toward the magazine well opening in the grip, insert the top of the magazine into the

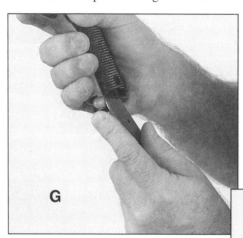

magazine well in the frame (G). Seat the magazine fully by pushing it all the way in with the palm of your hand, being sure to keep the trigger finger outside the

trigger guard (H). You will usually hear or feel a click as the magazine seats and is caught by the magazine catch. Once the magazine has been lined up with the magazine well and is being seated, return your visual focus to the target area.

If the pistol has been shot empty and the slide is locked back, release the slide forward by pulling the slide slightly to the rear and releasing it (I). If the gun being reloaded is not completely empty, there will be a round remaining in the chamber and no slide manipulation will be required. Note that a few semi-automatic pistols do not lock the slide back when shot empty. With such pistols, after a fresh magazine has been seated it will be necessary to fully retract the slide and release it to load a cartridge into the chamber and enable the pistol to fire.

After seating the magazine and releasing the slide forward, if necessary, the left hand slides back into its supporting position and the firing position is resumed (J).

During reloading, the eyes should remain continuously on the target or area of expected threat except for the brief moment when the magazine is being aligned with the frame. If the threat has fled or is otherwise gone when visual focus is returned to the target area, engage the safety and

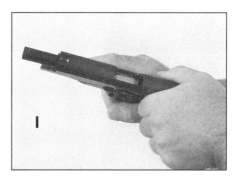

lower the pistol to a ready position.

# Reloading the Semi-Automatic Pistol (Left-Handed Technique)

Beginning with the pistol held in a firing grip, trigger finger indexed alongside the frame, and the muzzle pointed in a safe direction (A), bend the elbows to bring the pistol close to the body (B). The elbow of the shooting arm should be close to or in contact with the torso. The muzzle should point upward and away from you (or, if upward is not a safe direction, toward the target).

As you bring the pistol in close to the body, place the tip of the trigger finger on the magazine release button (assuming the button is located in the usual position on the left side of the frame just to the rear of the trigger guard). For some shooters, it may be necessary to use the stronger middle finger instead. Press the magazine release button straight into the frame and hold it in while the magazine drops free of the frame (C).You should be able

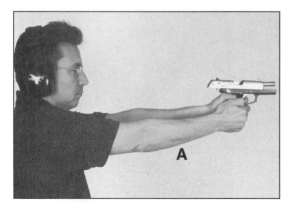

to glimpse the falling magazine in your peripheral vision. Do not attempt to retrieve the ejected magazine.

If your pistol has ambidextrous controls, it may be possible to release the magazine by pressing the release button with your left-hand thumb (D).

If the magazine does not fall free of the frame

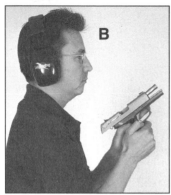

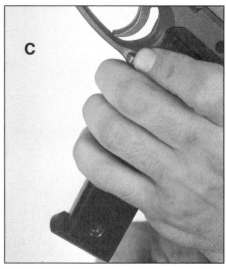

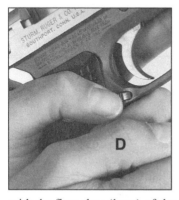

of its own weight, swiftly strip it from the pistol with the right hand and drop it on the ground.

At the same time as the spent magazine falls to the ground, the right (support) hand reaches for a fresh magazine (E). Grasp the magazine between the thumb and middle finger, with the floorplate (base) of the magazine in the palm of the hand and the index finger running up the front of the magazine body, resting on or just below the tip of the bullet of the top cartridge (F).

As the firing hand continues to bring the pistol in toward the torso,

The Basics of Personal Protection in the Home

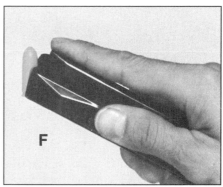

rotate the left hand wrist 90 degrees so that the right side of the frame faces you and the pistol is just below eye level (G). At the same time the right hand brings the magazine close to the magazine well of the pistol. Keep visual focus on the target area during theses steps.

Glance down at the magazine well, both to ensure that it is clear of an empty magazine and to locate it visually to facilitate magazine insertion (H). Using the right-hand index finger on the magazine to "point" toward the magazine well opening in the grip, insert the top of the magazine into the magazine well (I). Seat the magazine by pushing it all the way in with

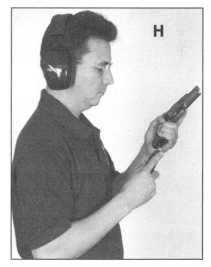

the palm of your hand, being sure to keep your finger outside the trigger guard (J). You will usually hear or feel a click as the magazine seats and is caught by the magazine catch. Once the magazine has been lined up

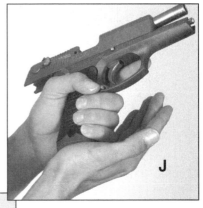

with the magazine well and is being seated, return your visual focus to the target area.

If the pistol has been shot empty and the slide is locked back, release

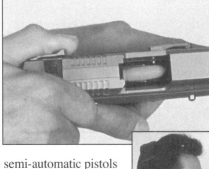

the slide forward by pulling the slide slightly to the rear and releasing it (K).

If the gun being reloaded is not completely empty, there will be a round remaining in the chamber and no slide manipulation will be required. Note that a few

semi-automatic pistols do not lock the slide back when shot empty. With such pistols, after a fresh magazine has been seated it will be necessary to fully retract the slide and release it to load a cartridge into the chamber.

After seating the

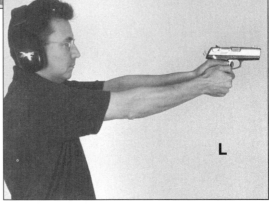

magazine and releasing the slide forward, if necessary, the right hand slides back into its supporting position, and the firing position is resumed (L).

During the reloading process, the eyes should remain continuously on the target or the area of expected threat except for the brief moment when the magazine is being lined up with the frame. If the threat has fled or is otherwise gone when visual focus is returned to the target area, engage the safety and lower the pistol to a ready position.

# CLEARING STOPPAGES

Your handgun is a tool of last resort, a tool you will avoid using unless you have no other options to safely stop an attack. However, when you must use your handgun, it must work reliably. The responsible gun owner will ensure that his or her firearm functions perfectly with the defensive ammunition selected.

No matter how much ammunition testing or gunsmith tuning is done, however, there still may be rare occasions when your handgun does not fire or otherwise fails to operate properly. Gun stoppages are somewhat more common with semi-automatic pistols, but can occur with revolvers, too. A gun stoppage that occurs during a violent encounter could render you helpless to stop an assailant's attack. For this reason it is important that you learn the *immediate action drills* for quickly clearing stoppages, and practice these drills until they are performed in an instantaneous, almost reflexive manner whenever a gun problem occurs.

# Clearing Stoppages in Open-Top Semi-Automatic Pistols

Many semi-automatic pistols have large, open-top ejection ports. Such pistols can be cleared of all three common stoppages—*failure to go into battery, failure to fire,* and *failure to eject*—using a single immediate action drill. From the point of view of the defensive shooter, being able to clear almost all stoppages with only one immediate action drill saves the time of having to analyze the malfunction, identify its cause and then decide which drill will remedy it. Having only one immediate action drill to learn and master also reduces training time and complexity, and enables you to be able to respond instantaneously anytime a stoppage occurs. The three steps of the drill are referred to as *tap, rack, assess.*

When a stoppage occurs, your trigger finger should be removed from the trigger (A). Next, tap the base of the magazine with the palm of the support hand to ensure it is fully seated in the pistol (B). Then, invert the pistol by rotating toward the thumb of the shooting hand. Rack the slide vigorously one time by pulling it all the way to the rear (C) and releasing it to go forward (D) under spring tension. Inverting the pistol before racking the slide and shaking the gun while the slide is momentarily held all the way back will dislodge all but the most stubborn empty case or jammed cartridge. Finally, assess the target to determine if it still constitutes a deadly threat.

Note that the tap, rack, assess drill will not work with all semi-automatic pistols. Experiment using only gross motor skills—which are

movements using the large muscles of the body—with various immediate action drills, using dummy ammunition or fired cases, to determine what works best with your handgun (see Chapter 12: Opportunities for Skills Enhancement).

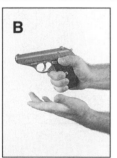
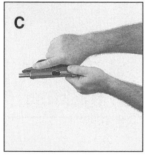
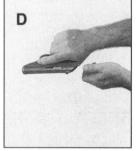

# Common Semi-Automatic Pistol Stoppages

There are several types of functional problems that may occur with semi-automatic pistols. The following stoppages are the ones most commonly experienced. Each may be resolved in one or two seconds utilizing the immediate action drill of tap, rack, assess.

**Failure to Go into Battery. (Next page; A, arrow)** This stoppage occurs

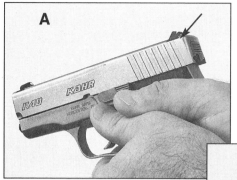

when the slide does not return all the way forward and the cartridge is not fully seated in the chamber. Most commonly this stoppage is caused by a round that gets jammed on the feed ramp leading into the chamber, an oversize or over-length cartridge, or an excessively dirty chamber.

**Failure to Fire.** Failure to fire can be the result of a cartridge defect, such as an improperly seated or defective primer, or a magazine that is not seated fully in the frame, which will prevent the slide from stripping and chambering the top cartridge. The most common stoppage is an empty chamber.

**Failure to Eject.** In this condition, the fired case is extracted at least partially from the chamber, but is not completely ejected from the pistol. The fired case may remain inside the slide, possibly becoming jammed into the chamber, or it may be partially protruding out of the ejection port. This latter condition is known as a *stovepipe* stoppage (B).

**Failure to Drop Magazine.** Defensive-oriented pistols generally are designed to drop their magazines freely when the magazine release is actuated. This promotes more rapid reloading, which may help save your life during a deadly attack. The failure to drop a magazine may have several causes. Most often a defective magazine (such as one that has a defective follower or is deformed so that it wedges inside the magazine well) is the culprit.

If this problem is observed during practice sessions with several magazines of good quality, it may result from a gun problem requiring a gunsmith's attention.

An empty magazine that does not drop free of the gun during the course of a defensive shooting situation must be immediately removed to allow reloading. The immediate action drill is to engage the protruding tongue of the magazine floorplate with the fingers of the non-shooting hand and, with the magazine release button depressed, sharply pull the magazine out of the gun (next page, A). Allow the magazine to drop to the ground.

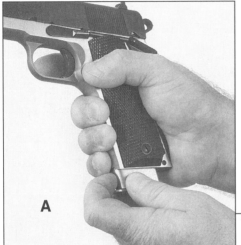

Note that some semi-automatic pistols feature magazine catches in locations other than the usual position just behind the trigger guard. The most common of these alternative locations is at the bottom of the pistol's butt (B). Such magazine catches require two hands for the release of a magazine, and consequently change the procedure for magazine

**A**

reloading detailed earlier.
**Feedway Clearance Immediate Action Drill.** If the tap, rack, assess immediate action drill fails to clear your pistol malfunction, immediately seek cover or distance. Lock open the canted slide if possible, then forcefully rip the magazine from the gun, retract and release the slide quickly until clear, but no more than three times and insert a fresh magazine, then tap, rack, and assess your target to determine if it still

**B**

constitutes a threat. You must never give up the will to prevail. If you cannot clear the malfunction, and your attacker remains a threat, consider using the gun as a

bludgeoning
device, or escape if
you are able to.

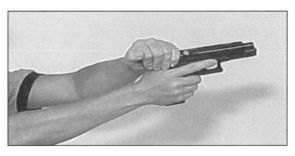

# Clearing
# Specific
# Revolver
# Malfunctions

There are two main types of functional problems that may occur with
revolvers.

**Failure to Fire.** A failure to fire with a revolver occurs whenever the
hammer falls on a loaded chamber (or what is thought to be a loaded
chamber) and the gun does not fire. The most likely cause for a failure to
fire in a stressful situation is that all the rounds in the cylinder have been
exhausted, and you have lost count of the number of shots you have fired.
Another cause for a failure to fire is that the hammer has fallen on a
chamber that does not contain a cartridge. This situation may occur when
reloading with loose cartridges under stress; it is easy under such
conditions to fail to fully load the cylinder.

On occasion the hammer may fall on a live round and fail to fire it. If
this occurs with ammunition
that has previously proved
reliable, this failure to fire is
most commonly the result of a
dud cartridge, a hangfire or
misfire. If this occurs at a
range while practicing, you
should wait 30 seconds with
the muzzle pointed
downrange, in the event that
the condition you are
experiencing is a hangfire. On
the other hand, if you are
using your handgun in a
defensive situation, you will
not have the luxury of holding
your fire for that period of
time. If you experience a
failure to fire during a
defensive shooting situation,

Fig. 62. A faint firing pin indentation (left case) can
result in a failure to fire, and may be a sign of a
firearm problem requiring a gunsmith's attention.

the proper immediate action drill is to pull the trigger again, bringing a fresh (and hopefully functioning) cartridge in line with the firing pin.

If the firearm fails to fire a second or third fresh round, open the cylinder and look at the primers of the cartridges that failed to ignite. A faint firing pin indentation [Fig. 62, left cartridge case, compared to a normal firing pin indentation on the right], or no indentation at all on an unfired primer is an indication of a firearm problem (such as a broken firing pin) that requires the intervention of a gunsmith.

**Failure to Eject Cases from the Cylinder.** Difficulty in ejecting fired cases from a revolver cylinder may result from oversized or high-pressure cartridges, dirt in the chambers or

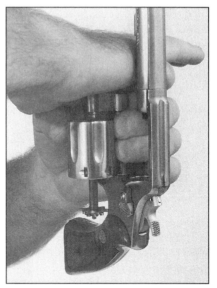

*Fig. 63. If your first strike of the ejector rod fails to eject all the cases from the cylinder, strike it again with greater force. Be careful to strike in a straight line to prevent bending it.*

roughly machined chambers. If this problem is encountered during practice sessions, a gunsmith's assistance should be sought to eliminate it.

A failure to eject cases that occurs during a violent encounter can prevent you from reloading your revolver, with dire consequences. If your first strike of the ejector rod fails to forcibly eject all cases from the cylinder, strike it again with greater force. Be careful to strike in a straight line with the rod to prevent bending it with an off-axis strike. If repeated strikes do not dislodge the cases, release the rod and use your fingers to pull the fired, partially-protruding cartridge cases from their chambers, one at a time.

# After Clearing a Stoppage

After clearing a stoppage in a semi-automatic pistol or a revolver, you must reassess the target to determine whether it still represents a deadly threat. In the brief moment it takes to conduct an immediate action drill, an assailant may surrender or flee. Conversely, while you are clearing a stoppage, an attacker may take the opportunity to advance on you. Avoid becoming so focused on your immediate action drill that you lose awareness of your attacker's actions. Furthermore, if your efforts to clear a stoppage become time-consuming, be sure to glance at the target area every second or two to maintain awareness of the threat.

# CHAPTER 12

# OPPORTUNITIES FOR SKILLS ENHANCEMENT

The NRA Basic Personal Protection in the Home Course should not be regarded as the endpoint of the training experience, but rather as the first step in the development of skills and abilities that will contribute to the personal safety of you and your family. There are many ways in which the knowledge, skills and attitude you have acquired in the Basic Personal Protection in the Home Course can be enhanced, from individual practice to formal training and official competition. The selection of the appropriate activity is based on your needs, resources and time schedule.

## DRY-FIRE PRACTICE

Dry-fire practice is an inexpensive, safe and time-efficient way to enhance shooting fundamentals, improve coordination and speed, and practice the various shooting positions. Dry-firing involves practicing every phase of the firing process using an unloaded firearm. All that is missing is the blast and recoil of an actual discharge.

All dry-fire practice must be performed in accordance with the following safety rules:

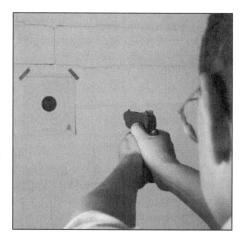

Fig. 64. Dry-fire practice can build skill away from the range. The firearm must be unloaded, and no ammunition should be in the dry-fire area. All gun safety rules should be observed, just as if the gun were loaded. Eye protection should also be worn.

• the firearm must be *completely unloaded;*
• all dry-firing is done in a dedicated dry-fire area having a safe backstop at which the gun is pointed;
• no live ammunition is allowed in the dedicated dry-fire area;

• if reloading drills are performed, only dummy ammunition is used; and
• eye protection must always be worn.

Of course, even though the firearm is unloaded, it is important to still observe the first basic rule of gun safety—*always* keep the gun pointed in a safe direction.

Dry-firing can be used to practice a variety of skills:
• reloading a revolver or semi-automatic pistol
• clearing stoppages (using dummy ammunition)
• assuming various shooting positions (barricade, kneeling, squatting, prone, etc.) from a standing ready position
• shooting fundamentals (aiming, breath control, hold control, trigger control and follow-through)
• grip, position and NPA (Natural Point of Aim)

The ways that dry-firing can be used to enhance your defensive shooting skills are limited only by your imagination. For example, you could set up several targets in a basement area providing a good backstop, and practice engaging the targets as you move from a standing ready position to other positions of cover. Maintaining a visual focus on the handgun's sights enables you to verify proper sight alignment and sight picture.

A variation on traditional dry-fire techniques has been afforded by laser technology. Several firms currently market target systems allowing a standard unmodified firearm to "fire" a burst of laser light at a target sensor, which emits a visual or audio signal when hit. These systems normally involve the insertion into the gun's chamber of a cartridge-shaped laser emitting unit that is activated by the strike of the firing pin. Such devices are especially useful in practicing point shooting and other non-aimed fire techniques.

# LIVE-FIRE PRACTICE

Although dry-fire practice, as well as the review of books, videos and other materials can add considerably to your knowledge and ability, there is no substitute for live-fire practice in improving defensive shooting skills.

Initially, the novice shooter should concentrate upon mastering the shooting drills presented in this course. Later, as both speed and accuracy improve, more challenging drills may be attempted. It is imperative that you

always observe the three main rules of firearm safety—*ALWAYS* *point the gun in a safe direction; ALWAYS keep your finger off the trigger until ready to shoot,* and *ALWAYS keep the gun unloaded when it is not in use*—during all live-fire exercises. Safety is never sacrificed or compromised for the sake of speed or for any other reason. If multiple target arrays are used, they must be positioned so as to allow all rounds fired to hit a suitable backstop.

It is often useful to have a shooting partner during live-fire exercises. Not only does this give you an additional incentive to practice; a shooting partner can help you better assess your progress. For example, a partner can time your exercises with a

*Fig. 65. Live-fire practice with a partner is an excellent way to build defensive shooting skill.*

stopwatch or an electronic shooting timer. The latter device is an especially useful tool. Typically, when the "start" button of a shooting timer is pressed, an audible "start" signal is emitted after a random 2- to 3-second delay. Each shot fired after the signal is sensed and timed by the device. After the particular string of shots is completed, you can review your times for each shot. Although a shooting timer is ideal for use with a shooting partner, you can also use it alone.

During a live-fire practice session, a shooting partner can also observe and give you feedback on your stance, grip, and shooting fundamentals. For a detailed, objective record of your practice session, have your partner videotape you while you shoot. (Always ensure that the video camera is behind the firing line, and that the camera operator is not exposed to danger from other shooters, ricochets, etc.) Videotape, especially when played back in slow motion, allows you to identify areas for improvement in your shooting form that the naked eye might miss.

# HOME DEFENSE SCENARIOS

In addition to assisting you during live-fire practice at the range, a shooting partner can also help you role-play various confrontational scenarios in your home. Typically, one person takes the role of the home defender, while the other is the attacker or intruder. *Never perform role-play exercises with an actual firearm, even though you know it to be unloaded. Always use a non-firing firearm simulator made for training use. These simulators are typically made of rubber or plastic and are brightly colored so as to be easily distinguishable from a real firearm. Never use a toy gun or a replica firearm.*

The possibilities of such role-play are almost limitless. For example, in a typical scenario the "defender," surprised by the "intruder," would put his or her defensive plan into action. Such a scenario might reveal flaws or limitations of the plan that should be corrected. In another exercise, the "intruder" could make various types of noises in different locations in the house to help the "defender" determine how easily a real intruder may be detected. Interestingly, the experience of persons doing such role play is that, even though they know it is only a pretend situation involving friends or family members, they will experience an elevated level of stress. Learning how to perform under such conditions will help better prepare you for the stress of a real encounter.

*Fig. 66. This couple is using a firearm simulator, a house key attached to a labeled piece of wood, and ideas from a magazine article to practice home defense scenarios.*

# WINCHESTER/NRA QUALIFICATION PROGRAM

You can develop your skills and gain recognition for your level of proficiency in the Winchester/NRA Handgun Qualification Program. The

The Basics of Personal Protection in the Home

*Fig. 67. The Winchester/NRA Qualification Program provides a graduated program of achievement in a recreational shooting activity.*

Program consists of six different skill ratings which are earned by attaining the required scores on a series of increasingly challenging courses of fire. Shooting is done with two hands and within specific time limits to help build shooting skills having real-world applicability. The Winchester/NRA Handgun Qualification Program is a self-paced recreational shooting activity that provides shooters of all skill levels with both fun and a sense of accomplishment. For more information on the Winchester/NRA Handgun Qualification Program, see Appendix C: Facts About the NRA.

# COMPETITION

Handgun competition is an excellent way to sharpen shooting skills, and the NRA offers matches open to beginner and expert alike. NRA Bullseye competition provides an opportunity to refine the shooting fundamentals—aiming, breath control, hold control, trigger control and follow-through—while NRA Action Pistol helps hone defensive skills by presenting varied target arrays that must be shot within relatively quick time limits. In most Action Pistol events, a large light-color target is used, with imprinted scoring rings in its center that are virtually invisible to the shooter. This helps the shooter develop the ability to accurately place shots in the center of target mass.

Practical handgun competition, such as that sponsored by IPSC

*Fig. 68. Match shooting helps sharpen gun handling and shooting skills under the pressure of competition.*

(International Practical Shooting Confederation), IDPA (International Defensive Pistol Association) and others, is a fun and exciting way to improve shooting and gun handling skills. In these sports, the shooter is presented with a virtually unlimited number of handgun challenges, and all firing is done against the clock. Most stages incorporate speed, movement and decision-making, thus giving the shooter practice in shooting accurately and quickly under stress.

For information on competing in NRA-sanctioned matches, as well as IDPA and IPSC competition, see Appendix B: Information and Training Resources.

## ADDITIONAL TRAINING

The NRA Basic Personal Protection in the Home Course provides a thorough grounding in the fundamentals of defensive shooting and home protection. Extensive practice and rigorous application of the techniques introduced in this course will make the shooter interested in home protection more capable of defending his or her life and family.

Some shooters, however, may wish to obtain additional training to learn new shooting techniques or increase their proficiency in the techniques already learned. These individuals can avail themselves of the training available at numerous facilities throughout the country. Note that the instruction provided at such facilities may vary in terms of length, quality, type and cost.

Shooters contemplating enrolling at such a facility to enhance their skills should consider at least the following factors:

- reputation of facility
- geographic location
- cost
- credentials of instructors
- student-teacher ratio
- safety record of institution
- types of courses offered
- availability of nearby lodging (for multi-day courses)

# EDUCATIONAL MATERIALS

In recent years there has been a great increase in educational materials related to defensive shooting. Today's shooter can choose from among hundreds of pamphlets, books and videos to gain information on virtually every aspect of gun ownership and use, from maintenance and disassembly to advanced firing techniques for self-defense and safe gun storage methods for the home. Appendix B: Information and Training Resources contains a sample of the available materials.

*Fig. 69. This sample of NRA materials related to firearms, firearm use, and personal protection represents a small fraction of the materials currently available from many sources. You are urged to glean as much information as possible from a wide variety of sources, including those outside the NRA, but always with a critical eye toward the effectiveness and safety of the techniques being taught.*

Note that the NRA does not necessarily approve or endorse the information contained in any of the materials listed in Appendix B. While much of the content of those materials is in agreement with official NRA training guidelines and policy, some content may differ from what is taught in NRA courses. You are urged to glean as much information as possible from a wide variety of sources, but always with a critical eye toward the effectiveness and safety of the techniques being taught.